THE SUBLIME *wedding*

you & your
wedding

THE SUBLIME
wedding

Finishing Touches for a Perfect Day

CAROLE HAMILTON

COLLINS & BROWN

For Nick and George

First published in Great Britain in 2004 by
Collins & Brown Ltd
The Chrysalis Building
Bramley Road
London W10 6SP

An imprint of **Chrysalis** Books Group plc

You & Your Wedding magazine is a trademark of the
National Magazine Company.
Published in association with the National Magazine
Company Limited.

Project Manager: Nicola Hodgson
Proofreader: Julie Jones
Designer: Zeta Jones

Distributed in the United States and Canada by Sterling
Publishing Co.
387 Park Avenue South, New York, NY 10016, USA

10 9 8 7 6 5 4 3 2 1

British Library Cataloguing-in-Publication Data:
A catalogue record for this title is available from the
British Library.

ISBN 1–84340–153–3 (hb)

Reproduced by Classicscan, Singapore
Printed by SNP Leefung China

contents

Introduction

Congratulations, you are going to be married! You are also about to start planning the wedding of your dreams, which is where I hope I can offer my help. As the editor of *You & Your Wedding* magazine for the past ten years, I can justifiably say that that I know pretty much everything there is to know about organizing a wedding. I have met and been inspired by many of the best suppliers in the wedding business. I have also had the privilege of meeting hundreds of brides at every stage of their planning process, gaining valuable insight into what organizing a wedding in the real world actually entails. And most of all, how it is possible to arrange a beautiful wedding without having an unlimited budget.

In the past few years, the biggest influence on the modern wedding has been celebrities. Love 'em or hate 'em, it's hard to ignore them, and once they decide to tie the knot there is a media frenzy leading to million pound contracts for the rights to even see the pictures. Reading about the designer dress, the gourmet food and the rivers of the finest champagne, it is easy for the average couple to believe that it is money that makes a great wedding.

Well, I am delighted to tell you that, in my opinion, anyone can have a sublime wedding – because true wedding style is not all about money. A wonderful wedding is about love and respect and about stamping your personalities on the biggest and best party you will ever organize.

This brings me to why I thought *The Sublime Wedding* was such a good idea. I believe that a beautiful wedding is about

the details. Every decision, big or small, from the lettering on your invitations to the bows on your bridesmaids' shoes says something about your personal style. The successful wedding is about working as a team with your wedding suppliers to create the perfect day, outlining your vision then listening to expert advice at the same time as getting the most for your money.

As you go through this book you will find inspiration for every aspect of your wedding. I will show you how to define your own personal style and then use this to create the day of your dreams. Every chapter is accompanied by beautiful photographs on each aspect of the big day, from the simplest favours to the most elaborate table decorations.

In the final chapter I have included a very special 'Insider's Roladex', a listing of many of the UK's and the US's best wedding suppliers, services and websites that I have come across whilst editing *You & Your Wedding*. This is an invaluable resource that no bride will want to be without.

Whether you have two years to plan an extravaganza in a castle or six months to arrange a register office ceremony and stylish luncheon, I hope that *The Sublime Wedding* will make your journey a little smoother. During this planning marathon you will experience highs and lows and, at times, need the patience of a saint to ensure everything comes together on time and on budget. But come together it most certainly will, so relax and remember to keep smiling. Because no matter what, this is your big day and you should enjoy every single moment!

THE ESSENTIAL *wedding checklist*

EVERYTHING YOU need to do ... and when you need to do it. This handy countdown takes you step-by-step through all of the major decisions you need to make during the wedding planning process as well as the ideal time to book the wedding dream team. Keep a photocopy of this checklist in your wedding file and tick off everything as it is sorted.

The average engagement is around 14 months but some couples have a lot longer and some only have a few months. If you have lots of time then finding your ideal venue and booking your first choice of supplier shouldn't be a problem. If you have less time you may need to be more flexible, perhaps rethinking the date or changing the wedding from a Saturday to a Friday for example, when suppliers are less likely to be busy (and often offer a better rate!). Couples on a tight schedule may find the services of a wedding organizer invaluable. They will have lists of venues and suppliers at their fingertips and have effectively done the shopping for you so will be able to suggest the right companies to suit your requirements.

There is no such thing as early when it comes to weddings. Once you have made a decision, book it or someone else probably will!

A wonderful wedding takes careful planning and it's never too early to start getting organized. Make key decisions as soon as possible and begin meeting suppliers anything up to a year in advance.

As Soon as Possible

- Tell relatives and close friends of your plans to marry.
- If required, place an announcement of your engagement in the local paper.
- Start a wedding file with pockets for swatches, tearsheets and lots of blank pages for names, addresses and details of suppliers.
- Arrange the first meeting with your minister, priest or rabbi to discuss the wedding plans and to set the date.
- If it's a civil ceremony, book the register office or civil venue and pay for the wedding licence.
- Set a budget and decide who is going to be paying for what. These days it is likely to involve joint funding between the couple and both sets of parents. A separate wedding bank account is a good idea.
- Make a list of your main wedding support team. You cannot possibly do everything yourself, so expect to delegate some of the major tasks to the groom, your mums and best friends. Alternatively, think about using the services of a wedding organizer.
- Decide on your bridesmaids, best man and other attendants.
- Decide on the ideal number of guests and begin to draw up the guest list with both sets of parents.
- If you are planning a summer wedding, consider sending out save-the-date cards so your guests are not on holiday.
- Visit possible reception venues.
- Discuss possible menus and gather estimates for the food and drink from various sources (caterer, off-licence etc). Arrange a tasting of the possible menu and sample the wines.
- Make all reception bookings, including the entertainment, in writing.
- Choose and then book your photographer and videographer, if you are having one.
- Take out wedding insurance, just in case. The average policy costs about a relatively small amount and covers you for just about everything.
- Begin looking for your wedding dress and attendants' outfits. Expect to pay a deposit for your dress when you have made your final decision. Buy your wedding lingerie and really wear this to all dress fittings.
- Start a beauty regime for hair, skin and nails.

Three Months

- Arrange a second meeting with the minister, priest or rabbi to discuss the service and agree a date for the publication of the banns. If the wedding is in a church other than the Church of England (in the UK), notice of the marriage must be given to the superintendent registrar.
- Select hymns and musical choices, book any musicians for the ceremony. Remember that anything for a civil wedding can have no religious references at all check with your registrar if you are unsure.
- Sample and then order the wedding cake.
- Order the wedding stationery, giving the printer a typed template with all spellings, dates and timings checked.
- Choose the florist and discuss requirements for the ceremony and reception.
- Arrange a schedule of wedding dress fittings.
- Think about organizing a creche for smaller guests or booking a child's entertainer.
- Discuss hairstyles and book a series of appointments with your hairdresser.
- Spend an afternoon with a travel agent and book the honeymoon.
- Book the honeymoon suite in a first night hotel, if different from the reception venue.
- Check passports are valid and arrange any necessary innoculations.

- If you are changing your name, visit the post office to complete the correct forms to change the name in your passport.
- Choose your wedding rings. Think about getting them engraved with your wedding date.
- Book all the wedding transport.
- Organize a gift list through a department store or specialist gift list shop.

Two Months

- Finalize the order of service and send a copy to the priest or registrar to ensure that everything is acceptable and the running order is correct.
- Order printed versions of the order of service sheets, allowing at least 20 spare copies.
- Reconfirm all prior bookings, double checking all dates.
- Post wedding invitations 8–10 weeks prior to the big day, including details of the gift list.
- Buy the bridal accessories, including shoes, veil and jewellery.
- Find affordable accommodation close to the reception to suggest to out-of-town guests.
- Choose favours for your guests, buy disposable cameras, wedding crackers, balloons and any other details/decorations you will need for the reception.
- Think about thank you gifts for the bridesmaids, best man, ushers and both mums.
- The groom should organize his clothes, arranging suit hire if necessary for himself and the main bridal party.

Two to Three Weeks

- Confirm the number of guests with your caterers and draw up a seating plan for the reception.
- Reconfirm all bookings made with venues, photographers, transport and entertainers.

- Order traveller's cheques and currency for the honeymoon.
- Inform banks, your employers, doctors, the tax office etc in writing if you are changing your name or names.
- Practise wedding make-up and hairstyle. Polaroid the finished look to ensure you are happy with how it looks on film.
- Wear your bridal shoes around the house to break them in.
- Draw up a play list of favourites (and music you dislike) to give to the band/disco who are providing the evening entertainment. Practise more than a shuffle for your first dance together.
- Enjoy the hen and stag celebrations.

One Week

- Arrange a rehearsal at the church, if applicable, to run through the ceremony with the officiant.
- Collect your wedding dress and store, hanging up in a large dress bag to prevent creasing.
- Finalize all details with the venue, florist, cake maker, transport and photographer. Type out a schedule of all timings and give one of these to all your main suppliers plus the best man and chief bridesmaid.
- Type out a list of all must-take photographs for the photographer including shots of you getting ready, leaving the house, with parents, special relatives and friends etc. Give a copy of the list to the best man or other trusted person to ensure nothing is missed during the day.
- Ensure the groom, best man and your dad are preparing speeches. Think about saying a few words yourself.
- Write notes to both sets of parents thanking them for their input into the wedding. Post them the day before the wedding so they arrive just after you have left for your honeymoon.

- Treat yourself to a professional facial and a massage so you are feeling refreshed and relaxed.

The Day Before

- Have a manicure and a pedicure.
- Pack for the honeymoon and arrange for the cases to be sent to the first night hotel.
- Relax and have an early night.

On The Day

- Give yourself plenty of time to get ready – you don't want to rush.
- Have something to eat, like a boiled egg and toast, you probably won't eat much at the reception.
- The bouquets and buttonholes should be delivered or send someone to collect them from the florist.
- The mother-of-the-bride plus any bridesmaids traditionally leave first, followed by the bride and her dad. The groom and best man make their own way to the ceremony and should aim to arrive at least 20 minutes before the bride.
- It is the best man's job to ensure all guests have transport between the ceremony and the reception. Therefore he should be one of the last to leave the ceremony.
- The reception is traditionally followed by the speeches. The bride's father speaks first, then the groom and then the best man. If the bride is going to speak, this is usually before the groom. The speeches are followed by the cutting of the cake.
- Traditionally the bride and groom left the reception first before their guests, the bride tossing her bouquet as she got into the car. These days, it is more usual for the couple to be staying at the reception venue and to party into the night with their guests before meeting them all again for breakfast the next day.

CHAPTER 1

SETTING YOUR *wedding style*

GETTING MARRIED IS hugely exciting and you are likely to spend most of your engagement in a whirl of anticipation. But in all the excitement of becoming engaged, it is easy to rush headlong into making decisions whilst you are in a heightened state of euphoria. So slow down and start planning like a professional.

To start your wedding preparations make a list of everything that will make your dream day complete. Do you see small and intimate, or a sit-down meal for 200? Will the ceremony be religious or civil? Once you have it all on paper, you can work out whether you can afford the dream.

Next you need to set the date, or at least the month when you would like to marry. Spring and summer are the most popular choices simply because the weather tends to be better. But winter weddings have a lot going for them, particularly in venues which lend themselves to romantic candlelight. Remember, many of the best venues get booked early so start making enquiries as soon as you can.

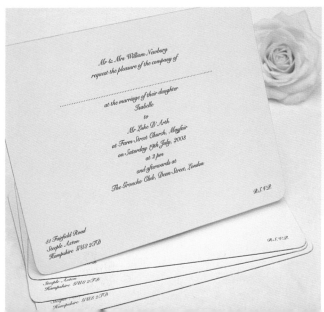

The invitations set the tone for your entire wedding and are the first indication your guests will receive of the overall style and formality of the occasion.

'The *perfect marriage* *begins* when each partner believes they got *better than* they *deserve*'

What Type of Ceremony?

The first big decision you will have to make is what type of marriage ceremony you want.

You basically have three options for marriage in England and Wales: a church ceremony, a civil wedding in a licensed building or a civil wedding in a register office. If you are at all unsure about which ceremony is right for you, make appointments with your church minister and with the local registrar to discuss your options. Alternatively, you may like to think about marrying overseas. Call the weddings department of one of the major tour operators, who will fill you in on all the legalities. (See pages 124–142 for contact details for the main religious denominations).

A church wedding: If you have opted for a church wedding, so long as you are both free to marry and live in the parish or are on the electoral roll, you may marry in the local parish church. **A civil wedding:** This can be held in any building with a wedding licence. There are currently more than 3000 licensed properties in the UK and you can obtain a full listing by contacting your local authority. The other type of civil wedding ceremony is held at the local register office and involves a quick and simple ceremony which can be booked up to 12 months in advance.

Requirements for marriage in the USA vary from state to state but basically involve a marriage licence and a ceremony, which can be carried out just about anywhere, including your own home. To receive a marriage licence you should check with your city's marriage bureau at the clerk of court's office to find out what is involved. You'll typicallly need to apply at least one month before the ceremony and your application needs to be witnessed so take along your bridesmaid or best man. Once you have the licence a marriage ceremony can be conducted by a number of officiants including a minister, marriage officer, judge or mayor. For more details see www.usmarriagelaws.com

Legally binding

To be legally married in the UK you must fulfil a number of requirements:

- You and your fiancé must be at least 16 years old (in England and Wales if either of you is under 18, written consent must be obtained from a parent or guardian)
- You must not be closely related
- The marriage must take place in premises where marriage can be legally solemnized
- The ceremony must take place in the presence of a registrar or other authorized person
- The ceremony must take place between 8am and 6pm (except for Jews and the Society of Friends)
- Two witnesses must be present
- You must both be free and eligible to marry

The wedding ceremony is a deeply moving event, as well as a legal undertaking. Think carefully about what will suit you best before making any final decisions.

MONEY TALKS

Once you have decided on the type of ceremony you want you can begin to think about the overall wedding style. This is also the time to think about setting the wedding budget.

Traditionally, the bride's parents paid for pretty much all of the wedding. But these days, with couples getting married later in life and probably already living together, it is much more usual for them to pay for their own wedding, with a contribution from both sets of parents.

It may not sound very romantic but you have to set a realistic budget and then stick to it. There is certainly nothing romantic about starting married life in debt. The best weddings are not always the most extravagant.

*Every little detail says something about your wedding style, from the mini umbrella name tags, **above**, to a full blown traditional reception, **below right**. Decide on the level of formality you want for your guests and then tailor everything else to suit this.*

Setting a theme

The most co-ordinated weddings usually follow a theme of some kind. Setting an overall style for all your suppliers to follow will help to keep costs down too. Here are some popular suggestions:

- A colour theme. Traditionally white and gold, white and silver, white and red, shades of pink or black and white.
- A historical theme. Let the history of your venue set the dress code and style.
- A seasonal theme. Pastels for spring, tea parties for summer, harvest golds for autumn, a christmas theme or pure white for winter.
- A military theme – if either of the couple are service personnel.
- A romantic or theatrical movie theme such as *The Great Gatsby*, *Pride and Prejudice* or *Dangerous Liaisons*.

If you would like your guests to dress to suit your theme, add a line to your invitations but don't be too disappointed if some guests stick to traditional wedding attire – dressing up doesn't suit everyone.

With imagination you can create a wonderful day on any budget. And it's often the little touches that your guests will remember most, such as innovative place settings or a moving reading at the ceremony.

List all of the components of your ideal wedding in order of priority. If a lavish reception is a must then you may have to rethink the honeymoon, and so on. All but the most expensive weddings involve compromise somewhere along the line. It is also a good idea to set up a separate wedding bank account and put all contributions into one fund so you can easily monitor what is being spent. Don't let unexpected expenses spoil your day. Add a 'miscellaneous expenses' category to your initial budget. Most couples go over their budget by about 5% and this safety net will mean you won't be scrimping once the honeymoon is over.

OOZE STYLE … ON A BUDGET
20 ways to have the most glamorous wedding without breaking the bank

1. Handle all your supplier negotiations like an adult. If you're afraid to haggle, you just won't get good deals. Don't be bamboozled by professional suppliers – stand your ground and only sign a contract when all the details meet your approval.

2. If any friends have got married recently, ask them about bargains they found. Check out local wedding shows for one-stop shopping all under one roof.

3. Summer is peak wedding season and everything to do with a wedding is more costly as you are competing with other couples for venues and services. Winter weddings often cost less yet still have a very elegant atmosphere.

4. Glamour means having the confidence to do things your own way. Consider a Friday evening, a midweek party or an elaborate Sunday event. Many venues offer discounts for weekdays and Sundays.

Above Tiny fresh flower posies add the prettiest touch tied to the plainest chairs. *Left* Thread coloured beads onto fine wire for inexpensive but trendy napkin holders. *Right* Nothing is as romantic as candlelight, these votives can double as name tags and favours for your guests too.

5. If you don't mind extra work, hire an empty venue and bring in your own suppliers for real savings. It does mean additional planning but you won't be limited to a venue's 'approved suppliers' list.

6. A morning or afternoon wedding usually means big savings. The limited hours will reduce your food and drinks budget. An afternoon tea party with champagne or a trendy cocktail party with canapes will impress your guests and cost a fraction of a formal sit-down meal.

7. Many charges are calculated on a per guest basis, so keep your wedding small. Treat it like a celebrity party and only invite 'A' list friends and relatives.

8. To cut corners without cutting the glamour, think simplicity. Fussy, expensive details, often look 'cheaper' than something plain.

9. Suggest your bridesmaids wear cocktail party dresses rather than traditional and expensive bridesmaids outfits. For smaller maids, check out the high street department stores which have fantastic deals on party dresses.

10. To save money on flowers, select in-season flowers. If there is one special flower that you simply must have, limit this to just your bridal bouquet.

11. A church ceremony can mean free flowers near Easter or Christmas. And a civil wedding venue may already be decorated with holly, candles and a Christmas tree for a December wedding.

12. Ask your florist to take some arrangements from your ceremony to the reception. They can be rearranged while everyone is enjoying a drink in another room.

13. Candles and nightlights create a very romantic atmosphere at a fraction of the cost of flowers. Use bowls of water and floating candles or flower petals for modern centrepieces. Put tealights onto window sills and mantlepieces and dim overhead lighting as evening draws in.

14. Check corkage charges at your reception venue and see whether it makes financial sense to bring your own drinks. Travelling to France to buy wine and champagne is inexpensive and providing it is for your own consumption, you can buy as much as you like.

15. Don't dismiss a buffet reception as being 'downmarket'. Food stations offering tastes from lots of different countries are very fashionable and can save money.

16. For an evening party, fill punch bowls with a cocktail named after the bride and groom rather than having an unlimited free bar.

17. Alternatively, a cash bar is generally expected these days, so don't feel guilty about asking guests to pay for drinks once the formal part of the reception is over. Putting money behind the bar for the first round is a nice touch.

18. Supplement a small, elaborate wedding cake with plain cakes hidden in the kitchen for serving to guests once the cutting ceremony is over.

19. Serve your wedding cake as dessert for extra savings. Modern cakes are often a concoction of chocolate and fruit and with the addition of a little cream or fruit coulis make the perfect pudding.

20. Consider using a wedding organizer, particularly if you don't have lots of time to shop around. For an often reasonable fee they have contacts with everyone from venues to florists and can arrange discounts and deals with favoured suppliers.

WHAT TYPE OF BRIDE ARE YOU?

Check out below to see which style of wedding best suits your personality

The Shrinking Violet

Personality: You're warm and loving but a bit on the shy side. You're not comfortable being the centre of attention.

The Look: Your wedding style is subtle but pretty. A meaningful ceremony followed by a country garden reception is ideal. You love flowers so these will play a big part in every aspect of the day.

Style Tips: A pile of individual fairy cakes will suit your unaffected style. A barn dance or ceilidh will create a relaxed and not too formal atmosphere for your guests. Packets of wildflower seeds or mini pot plants are your ideal favours.

Miss Romantic

Personality: As a little girl you wished upon a star for a fairytale wedding will all the trimmings. Just don't forget that Prince Charming needs to play a part in his own wedding, you'll need to come down off cloud nine occasionally to avoid pre-wedding tension.

The Look: Your dream setting is a castle and you will want to wear a ballgown-style dress complete with a princess tiara and Cinderella slippers. Old fashioned roses in pink or white are your ideal flowers.

Style Tips: Hearts, cupids and fairies should adorn everything from the invitations to the place settings. Treat your guests to traditional favours: five sugared almonds representing health, wealth, happiness, fidelity and prosperity. Release white doves as you leave the reception as a sign of everlasting love.

Suave Sophisticate

Personality: You were the little girl who was always dressing up in your mum's high heels. You like the finer things in life and you're secretly nostalgic for the days of glam movie stars like Grace Kelly and Audrey Hepburn.

The Look: Your wedding style is classically elegant with a nod to modern chic. You'll probably like a reception at a townhouse hotel or in marquee in the country. Every detail will be considered and your guests will know your perfectionist hand has been involved in everything.

Style Tips: Only a silver service reception will be good enough for you. Keep your drinks budget in check by serving trendy cocktails named after your favourite movie stars rather than champagne. End the evening with a spectacular fireworks display.

Miss Trendy

Personality: You are known as the life and soul of any party, and everyone loves you. You are endlessly creative and probably a bit chaotic, so you'll need to get organized early – or think about employing a wedding organizer to sort the main details.

The Look: Your wedding will be memorable because it is either a mad modern do or a themed extravaganza. You love colour and find plain and simple boring. Red, gold or hot pink are likely to be your colour themes.

Style Tips: Your guests will love food stalls offering a dazzling array of nibbles from sushi to mini hot dogs. Entertainment needs to be funky, perhaps a live soul band or the latest DJ. Employ roving artists or celebrity look-a-likes to mingle.

THE CONTEMPORARY *wedding*

WHITE · LIME · MINIMALIST · MODERN · SWAN LAKE · FEATHERS

NATALIA KUDIMOVA AND VIOREL CAMPEANU at The Hempel Hotel, London. 'We wanted a venue which was modern and stylish, yet very beautiful. The Hempel is all white and light floods in through the tall windows creating a romantic atmosphere. Our overall theme for the day was Swan Lake. We had a fantastic ice sculpture of two swans sitting on the pond in the gardens, our wedding cake was a swan made from profiteroles and white chocolate and we gave our guests miniature marzipan swans in white boxes as favours.

My bouquet was white cala lilies and white feathers and the bridesmaids had posies of pale pink roses. The reception tables were decorated with glass cubes of pale pink orchids, white feathers and slices of lime. We entered the gardens to greet our guests through a flower arch of pink orchids.

Just before the reception, the bridal party went on the London Eye which made a spectacular start to the day. Our guests were entertained by a classical quarter playing Tchaikovsky, and after dinner we danced to a firey gypsy band who played Russian and Romanian tunes, which reflected our cultures.'

Steal their wedding style

- Choose a contemporary venue if you like minimalist style
- Echo the venue with simple white table settings
- Cover plain chairs with white slipcovers tied with oversized organza bows
- Trim all flower arrangements with feathers, a very pretty but inexpensive detail
- For accents of colour in tablecentres, use fresh fruits like lime, lemon and orange
- Save on champagne and serve cocktails named after the bride and groom
- Serve an interesting fusion menu featuring flavourful tastes from around the world, Italian – Thai and Japanese are popular choices

'Our most memorable moment was releasing white doves to celebrate our union.'

CHAPTER 2

THE WEDDING
venue

WHAT IS YOUR dream wedding venue? A romantic castle, a beautiful stately home, a marquee in a country garden or a funky boutique hotel? The first step towards setting the style for your wedding is to find the perfect venue for your celebrations. Where you choose will be dictated by a number of factors, first and foremost, the type of marriage ceremony you have chosen. If it is a church wedding you will need to find a venue for the reception no more than 30 minutes travelling time from the church. The same applies if you are having a civil ceremony in a register office. If you are having a civil wedding in a licensed building you will have more choice, since both the ceremony and the reception are held in the same place.

You will also need to think about whether you want to marry close to where you are currently living or would feel happier returning to a venue closer to your childhood homes, which may suit the majority of your friends.

Discuss the type of wedding you want with your groom, bearing in mind the season, your budget and the level of formality you had imagined so that you are both looking for the same thing before you start making any decisions.

How many guests do you want to attend?
The size of your wedding will impact on your choice of venue. Many places have a restriction on numbers and if you are planning on more than 100 guests you may find your choices become limited. If you want to invite lots of children you need to find a child-friendly venue preferably with secure space outside for them to play.

The relaxation in the marriage law means that all manner of amazing venues are now available for civil wedding ceremonies. Everything from romantic castles and grand stately homes to chic big city hotels can be booked for a wedding to suit your dreams.

'Don't marry a person
you can live with,
marry someone
you can't live without'

How formal do you see your wedding?
A traditional drinks party followed by a sit-down lunch or dinner is the most formal option. A more contemporary reception is a buffet but still with chairs and tables for your guests. The most casual styles of reception are a finger buffet (where most guests remain standing), a barbeque or afternoon tea party. The level of formality you choose has a lot to do with your budget, since the more formal the occasion, the more expensive it usually becomes.

Where will suit your dream? If you have always dreamed of a country house wedding with your guests sipping champagne in the gardens, then this is what you should be planning. If the thought of such formality sends shivers up your spine then think about transforming a more contemporary setting. Or you may want something completely different, in which case there are hundreds of buildings which lend themselves to a themed wedding. Contact the local council for a list of venues in your area or see pages 124–143 for a selection of venue-finder websites.

As with every aspect of your wedding, do your research before booking anything. Request brochures from a wide selection of possible venues and draw up a shortlist to actually visit. When you are there, ask about capacity, menu options and, of course, whether the venue is available on your chosen date.

Many venues that host weddings offer a variety of wedding packages to suit all budgets, ranging from finger buffets to four-course dinners. Choosing one of these packages is the least complicated option since you know what is included in the price, just make sure you read all the small print. There are often hidden extras, with separate charges for items like linen and flatware. Take paperwork home to read in your own time. Never feel you have to sign anything on the spot without taking adequate time to reflect on all the details.

The choice of reception venue is all-important if it is to suit your wedding style. Visit a selection of possible locations and ask to see their portfolio of previous weddings to see if these inspire you. If you cannot find the perfect place, think about booking a marquee or large unfurnished room and then adding decorations to suit your chosen theme.

Questions to ask potential wedding venues

Q. Will you have the venue for sole use on the day?

Q. Is there in-house catering? Or can you use your own?

Q. Can they provide all tables, chairs, linens and the waiting staff?

Q. Is there an in-house florist?

Q. Can you and some of your guests sleep overnight at the venue?

Q. Do you have use of any gardens? Can you put up a marquee? Will this cost extra?

Q. Are there any restrictions on decorating the venue?

Q. Are there any noise restrictions? Can you set off fireworks?

Q. Are there any restrictions on the amount of electrical equipment your proposed entertainers can bring along, such as extra lighting for the disco, amplifiers etc.

Q. Is the parking adequate for the number of guests?

Q. Will there be a designated wedding manager on site throughout the wedding?

Q. How much is the deposit? When will the balance need to be paid?

THE VENUE STYLE

When you visit each venue remember to take a good long look at the way it is decorated and whether it will suit the proposed theme you have in mind. There is nothing you can do about existing wall coverings or the carpets, so make sure they won't clash horribly with your own ideas. Hotels and country houses tend to be ornately furnished making them unsuitable if you envisage a minimalist occasion.

If you are having a summer wedding, look at any patio areas and gardens to ensure they are clean and tidy. Are there umbrellas to provide shade for your guests or will you have to hire these separately? The size of the rooms also need to suit the number of guests you are having. The venue will be able to advise on the number of people they can accommodate for a sit-down meal. But if you are hosting a small wedding, you need to find a room that will create an intimate atmosphere. An overly large room, however lovely, will feel as if half your guests haven't shown up!

If you are the sort of bride with strong ideas about a themed reception and cannot find the ideal venue, hiring a hall is a good option. These usually have plain whitewashed walls so you can go to town adding your own decorations. It is relatively simple and inexpensive to arrange white muslin across windows, hire white furniture and then add splashes of colour with flowers. Turn off any harsh overhead lighting and use lots of candles to add instant atmosphere.

Once you have booked your venue, expect to receive a contract listing all the details agreed between you and the venue and all the costings. Before you sign, check that everything you discussed has been included. Adding extras at a later date is never cost-effective.

You will be asked to pay a deposit of around 20%, often non-refundable, when you book the venue. The balance of the money is usually payable when you confirm final guest numbers about a fortnight before the big day.

Before you book …

If you are having a civil wedding in a licensed premises, make sure the registrar is free on that date before booking the venue. Each council only has a limited number of registrars and during popular summer months they get very busy. I have heard of several couples having to forfeit their venue deposit because they couldn't get a registrar on their favoured date.

If you are planning a summer wedding remember to look at the grounds as well as the interior of the venue to ensure they suit your ideas. And remember to check that everything is child-friendly and safe for younger guests.

THE HOME WEDDING

Celebrating your wedding with a reception at your family home is a lovely idea, but be realistic. Think of the movie *Father of the Bride* and now imagine the same thing in your home. Unless your house is very spacious or you are having less than 50 guests, the average home probably is not big enough to accommodate anything but the simplest wedding party.

If you are planning a wedding at home, putting up a marquee is the obvious answer to space problems. Modern marquees come with hardwood floors and in a variety of sizes to suit just about any number of guests. A marquee also acts as the focal point of the celebrations, keeping guests to one location rather than traipsing all over your home.

Things to think about when organizing a wedding at home:

- You will need to hire caterers – can your kitchen cope?
- Will you need to hire tables, chairs, glasses, tableware and linens?
- How many staff will you need to hire? You need people to wait tables and serve food but also to clear everything away
- Will you need portable loos?
- Where will your guests park their cars?
- Do you have enough plug points for extra lighting and sound systems?
- What will you do if it rains?
- Can your fridge cope with making ice, chilling drinks?
- Do you, or your parents, have enough time to organize a home wedding or should you book a wedding planner?

THE HISTORICAL *wedding*

HISTORY · ROMANCE · ROSES · SUNSHINE · CLASSICAL MUSIC · TRADITION

KIM MASON AND NEIL SAWYERS at Amberley Castle, Sussex. 'We are a pretty romantic couple and had always dreamed of getting married in a castle. Amberley is spectacular and one of the oldest castles in Britain, with many parts dating back to 1103. It makes an amazing setting for a wedding.

The drive up to the castle is one most of our guests will never forget. You are greeted by the massive portcullis and beautiful gardens overflowing with flowers. The castle is an exclusive hotel and we had it to ourselves for the weekend with many family and friends staying overnight. Revisiting magic moments over breakfast the morning after the wedding was one of our favourite memories.

Our colour scheme was burgundy and cream roses, which was echoed through the bridal bouquet, reception tablecentres and venue decorations. The wedding breakfast menu was traditional English fare of smoked salmon, fillet of English beef with apple tart and homemade ice-cream for dessert. The bride's mother made our wedding cake which was decorated with sugar icing roses.

We used the services of a traditional toastmaster and had a juggler in full jester's costume to entertain our guests. The wonderful sounds of a classical harpist filled the castle during the reception.

The most memorable part of the day for us was seeing our guests having such a wonderful time.'

Steal their wedding style

- Choose a venue with a sense of history, like a hotel, country house or even the local pub
- Design invitations with an olde worlde theme and incorporate extravagant calligraphy
- Suggest a dress code, traditional attire like morning dress or dress to suit the theme in historical costumes
- Entertain guests with classical music from a string quartet or harpist. Employ a magician or a court jester to mingle with guests
- Candlelight is always romantic in a dramatic setting – hire a mixture of tall and small candelabras
- Make poetry and readings part of the the ceremony
- Name the reception tables after historical characters or important events from history.

'Our wedding was the epitome of a perfect English summer's day'

CHAPTER 3

YOUR DREAM *team*

Y OU'VE IMAGINED THE perfect wedding day hundreds of times – the fairytale dress, the gorgeous flowers, delicious wedding breakfast and your favourite songs playing as you dance with your new husband. But this wonderful dream will stay just a dream unless you assemble a team of experts around you to help turn the whole thing into reality.

You only have to hear one bride crying about her fuzzy photos, wilted bouquet or tepid food to realize you can't trust your day to just anyone. Experienced professionals are essential to any successful wedding. They will guide you as you form your ideas, add their own creative expertize and, most importantly, make it all happen on the day.

After you have decided on the basics such as the style, size, time and location of your wedding and reception, it is time to find a team of people whom you can trust to listen to you beforehand, co-operate with you during the planning stages and come through with flying colours on the wedding day itself.

A successful wedding is all about teamwork – not just between the bride and groom and their respective families but also with the wedding suppliers. Everyone from the florist to the catering manager at the reception venue will play a big part in the smooth organization of the whole day.

'*Happiness* is being
married to your *best friend*'

A good supplier will have creative ideas about how to get the most out of your money. If you feel someone is pressurizing you to spend more, save time and hassle and look elsewhere. Ask for photographs or recordings of previous work and samples to see, hear or taste.

Evaluate how well you get on with the potential suppliers. You'll be spending a lot of time together in the planning stages of the wedding and on the day, so you need to know that your personalities and your sense of style are compatible.

Before you sign anything, tread carefully. Get everything in writing the dates, times of delivery or performance, what products and services will be provided and the exact costs. Check all the small print thoroughly for hidden extras. Also specify in writing any named brands, types of flowers or food you are expecting. With chefs, photographers and musicians, ensure that the people you meet are the ones who'll show up on the day.

SHOP AROUND

Word of mouth recommendation from friends who have recently got married can be invaluable in your search for quality suppliers. If this is not available, request a list of references from all potential companies and phone each one to verify them. Ask for an honest rundown of the good and bad points, and whether the service was worth the money.

Once you've started hiring suppliers ask them for recommendations too. They work in the wedding world all the time and know who is reliable and, more importantly, who is not.

Before hiring anyone, get three different estimates. Look at the overall cost, but make sure you know what's included. Sometimes a higher price means they'll take on more responsibilities, freeing up your time and energy for other things.

At your initial meetings, don't mince your words. Be honest about your budget – and stick to it.

PHOTOGRAPHS AND VIDEO

The photographs and video of your wedding will be amongst your most cherished keepsakes and brides who try to scrimp on these are nearly always disappointed. Don't end up with badly lit photographs or a jiggly video shot by a friend. Trust a professional – you can't go back and do it all over again if you don't like the results. A professional will charge higher rates but, as always, you get what you pay for.

Photographers and videographers often get booked up well in advance, so it's important to find the right people as soon as possible. First, decide on the style you prefer. Do you like reportage photography that catches candid moments, formal posed portraits or a mixture of them both? Do you want all colour photographs or a mixture with black and white? Choose someone who specialises in the type of shots you prefer – reportage photography may look easy but it takes skill to capture 'unposed' moments well.

Styles of wedding photography

- **OLD-SCHOOL ROMANCE:** Not every bride wants avant-garde pictures. There's a lot to be said for traditional and shamelessly romantic shots, so long as they are not clichéd and the quality is excellent.

- **REPORTAGE OR STORY BOOK:** This candid style of photography is currently very popular. Photographers who specialize in this style are intent on capturing the impromptu moments to create a storybook feel to the day. From getting ready with your bridesmaids to the best man sneakily practising his speech behind the marquee, you'll have a real flavour of the day.

- **BLACK AND WHITE:** Even if you love colour pictures and spent hours co-ordinating everything so it matches perfectly, it is still a good idea to include a few rolls of black and white. With the ability to throw atmospheric contrasts of light and dark, they are a throwback to fifties photography and can look very stylish.

- **HAND-TINTING:** This is a special technique where the photographer enhances a black and white image with splashes of colour, for example, only the bouquet is in colour on a black and white shot.

- **SEPIA:** Instantly recognizable brownish or bluey shots, reminiscent of very early photography. White dresses appear ivory and these soft tones are generally very flattering. Some photographers shoot black and white and sepia, so you can mix them in your album.

- **DIGITAL IMAGING:** Modern computer technology allows shots to be digitally enhanced to your heart's desire, so brides and grooms can be superimposed against a fairytale background or have 'love' written across the sky. Digital imaging can also be used to clean up any blemishes or to enhance the colours in a print. If your photographer uses a digital camera, you can download the pictures onto a computer and e-mail shots to friends around the world.

If you're having a video, ask about background music, and special effects such as slow motion, which can make your video look like a feature film rather than a home movie.

When you inspect a photography portfolio, insist on seeing all the proofs from the particular wedding you are viewing, rather than a smattering of random, carefully selected shots. Watch an entire sample video of one wedding, not just a series of clips from several weddings.

Explain the running order of the day and list the events you want recorded especially any 'unmissable' shots. Ask how many hours they will work – some cover only the early events while others will stay to capture every moment.

Make sure that the photographer and videographer understand the role the other will play on the day and won't get in each other's way. Don't forget to ask about the payment plan, whether packages are flexible and whether you can keep the proofs.

THE FLORIST

Flowers play an essential part of any wedding and the key to the best wedding flowers is finding the right florist. Make a clippings book of bouquets and flowers you like – and those you don't – to give potential florists an exact idea of what you're looking for.

At your initial meeting it is also a good idea to take along a picture or sketch of your dress, along with fabric swatches for colour matching.

Looks at portfolios of previous work to see if their style matches yours. Describe the looks you're tying to achieve and ask for their input. An experienced florist should have dozens of helpful hints on bouquet shapes, specific flowers to match your colour scheme, creative centrepieces and ways to cut costs if that's what your budget demands. Most florists will be happy to mock-up the bridal bouquet and the tablecentres so you can see how their ideas are progressing.

If the florist hasn't worked at your venues before, be sure they can visit them before the event. Find out how much time your florist will have on the day to set up and decorate each room and how many helpers they will be bringing with them. Be sure that you are comfortable working together and that the florist respects your ideas and will be able to create designs you like within your budget.

Start your search for a florist about six–nine months before the wedding and expect to finalize all the details about three weeks before the big day.

Your florist is one of your most important suppliers, interpreting your ideas and helping to create the most beautiful day. A good florist will make clever use of colour as well as introducing decorative touches like co-ordinating ribbons, and interesting ways of displaying the flowers in everything from plain glass bowls to pretty sequinned bags.

THE CATERERS

The catering company is a vital member of your team. The food you serve your guests can make or break your reception and it is likely to account for the largest slice of your wedding budget.

First, decide what type of celebration you want – a cocktail reception, afternoon tea, sit-down meal or a buffet reception. Then work out your budget. As a general rule, the more formal the occasion, the more expensive it becomes.

There are two types of caterer, in-house based at the venue or off-site caterers who bring everything to your venue. Many venues offer wedding packages, ranging in price from a budget buffet to full silver service. Most also include the use of tables, chairs, china, cutlery, waiting and bar staff costed on a 'per guest' basis. Alternatively, you can list everything you want and the caterers and venue come up with a price for individual items.

You will want your guests to be well fed but this doesn't have to mean a formal sit-down meal. Interesting canapes with cocktails or afternoon tea parties are equally welcome and provide cost-conscious alternatives that are memorably stylish.

If you are having a home wedding or holding your reception in a venue that needs completely furnishing, there are any number of hire companies you can use offering everything from plates and cutlery to fancy chairbacks, fake flower garlands, mini ovens and heaters (see pages The White pages section at the back of the book for suggestions).

Once you have drawn up a shortlist of caterers, ask for a tasting session of the proposed menu and drink options. Discuss whether there is a minimum number of guests required, overtime rates and when you need to provide a final head count. Specify all these details in a contract and expect to pay anything up to 50% of the total cost when you book.

MUSIC AND ENTERTAINMENT

Music is the soundtrack of your wedding day, so you want it to be just right. Before looking for musicians for the ceremony or reception, check with your officiant and the reception venue about style or time restrictions and allowable decibel level. Let potential performers know how many guests are coming and where you want them to play. With their experience they'll know how many musicians and what sound equipment to use.

Recommendations from friends can help you to find the right musicians, but when you've narrowed down your search still insist on seeing the performers live if possible. At least see a video of a wedding performance. Specify the style of music you'd like at the reception, but remember that you can't ask a band to stray too far from its speciality.

Whether you have a live band or a DJ, agree to a playlist of tunes you love. If Celine Dion sends the wrong kind of shivers down your spine, make this clear. Many wedding bands have a standard repertoire so have a look at their suggested list and delete any songs you detest.

If you're hiring a DJ, be sure to make clear whether or not you want him to chat between songs and whether or not you think his mirror ball, lighting and props are appropriate for your style of celebration. For all performers, specify arrival and departure times, the timing of breaks, provision of food and drink and a suggested dress code. Black trousers and white shirts, or a black dress is a safe and professional looking option for any style of occasion.

Take into consideration the ages of all your guests before deciding on the entertainment at your reception – there is nothing worse than an empty dance floor. Many couples choose a mixture of live music and a DJ to vary the musical styles and to suit all tastes.

THE WEDDING ORGANIZER

More and more couples are turning to a professional to organize some or all of their wedding. These wedding planners are experts in managing all the suppliers and venues and often have great contacts, saving you money by guiding you in the right direction to suit your budget.

If you have a demanding job and want to enjoy your weekends rather than spending every waking moment meeting potential suppliers, a professional planner can be a life saver. They are also invaluable if your wedding is in a different town from where you live. And they're absolutely essential if you're bursting with creative ideas but logistical realities elude you. A professional will help tie up all the loose ends and ensure everything runs smoothly throughout the day – so you can relax and enjoy the wedding.

You may need a wedding organizer if ...

• Your wedding venue is at the other end of the country from your home.
• You have a high pressure job and not enough time to organize details.
• You get easily daunted by the thought of planning a family party – admit it, a wedding will be a nightmare.
• You are having so many arguments with your fiancé and family that it would be simpler to let someone else make the decisions.
• You find negotiating prices with suppliers difficult or embarrassing.
• You haven't a clue where to start – on anything at all.

And not forgetting friends and family

Many of the stressed-out brides I have talked to over the years have one thing in common, they are invariably trying to do everything themselves. And whilst they are slowly turning into the infamous Bridezilla, their family and friends are feeling hurt because they have been left out of the wedding preparations!

Learn the art of delegation. Once the guidelines have been set you should be able to pass on key tasks to trusted members of your wedding team – not to mention your groom who is probably feeling completely left out of his own wedding.

Seek out friends with particular skills. A great organizer is perfect for monitoring the gift list. Your mum would probably like to organize the RSVPs from the guest list. Get your groom involved with the food and drink as well as the entertainment. Don't be afraid to ask for help, chances are everyone is itching to have their input and will be delighted to be asked.

As the weeks move on you can meet up with each person for a progress report, ensuring that everything is just how you want it – it's still your wedding after all!

The fine print

When it comes to a wedding there's no room for error and the right paperwork goes a long way in helping to ensure the professionals you have employed come through on the day. Every bride needs to be clear cut about what they want and to confirm everything in writing. Read everything carefully and don't sign until you are completely satisfied. Be sure to include all the basic details like names, addresses, dates, venues, services to be provided, timings, costs – including VAT – and agreed extras. Last but not least, take out wedding insurance. Keep a copy of all receipts and correspondence plus proof of any payments made for deposits. Insurance will add little to your overall budget and whilst it cannot make a disappointing day perfect, it can offer financial compensation to ease the pain.

THE WEDDING TIMETABLE

A few weeks before the big day, work out an approximate wedding timetable, detailing what time you would like everything to start and finish. Be realistic, you don't want to feel that your wedding is running behind schedule all day. On the other hand, don't allow too much time between each part of the day otherwise you are in danger of your guests becoming bored. Make sure that key suppliers like the banqueting/catering manager, the florist and any entertainers have a copy of your timetable well beforehand so they know what you are expecting.

Here is an approximate timetable for an average ceremony followed by a traditional wedding reception:

3.00pm Ceremony Arrivals

Groom and best man arrive first to greet guests as they arrive at the venue. Ushers hand out an order of service to each guest and direct them to their seats. Friends of the bride seated on the left, friends of the groom on the right.

The bride and her father arrive last, their entrance heralds the start of the ceremony.

3.30–4.00pm Ceremony

Depending on whether it is a religious or civil service the ceremony takes from about ten minutes to half an hour.

4.00-4.30pm Photographs

Time for a selection of photographs of the bride and groom leaving the ceremony and then surrounded by friends and family at the venue. The best man and ushers ensure that all guests have transport to the reception. The bride and groom, bridesmaids and parents leave first.

5.00pm Reception Arrivals

The wedding party arrives at the reception, before the guests if possible.

5.00–5.30pm The Receiving Line

The bride and groom and the main wedding party form a receiving line. If you're not having one, this is a good time for photos of the bride and groom alone. Just make sure your guests are welcomed with a glass of champagne.

5.30–6.15pm Cocktails

Welcome drinks are typically held away from the main dining room. Plenty of drinks and hors d'oeuvres are essential. Guests can check the seating plan and newlyweds can circulate.

6.15–6.30pm Announcements

Dinner is announced by the head waiter or a toastmaster if you are having one. The wedding party enter the dining area first to find their tables. If the bride and groom choose to be announced, they make their grand entrance once their guests are seated.

6.30pm Welcome

Once the bride and groom are seated and the room has calmed down, the father-of-the-bride or a toastmaster welcomes the guests. A minister or parent may say a blessing.

6.40pm Dinner

The first course is served to the wedding party and then to all guests along with the wine.

7.00pm Courses

The first course is cleared from the top table first, then the guests' tables. Other courses follow in good, but not rushed, time.

8.30pm Toasts

After dessert, guests' flutes are topped up with champagne. The bride's father toasts the health of the bride and groom.

8.35pm Speeches

The father-of-the-bride makes the first speech and is followed by the groom, who responds for himself and his wife and proposes a toast to the bridesmaids. The groom may also give small thank-you gifts to the bridesmaids at this stage. The best man replies on behalf of the bridesmaids and his speech follows. If the bride wants to say a few words, she can do this before, or at the same time as her groom.

9.30pm The Cake

The newlyweds cut the cake, which is then served with coffee.

10.00pm First Dance

The bride and groom take to the floor for their chosen first dance. The next dance is reserved for the bride and her father and the groom and his mother. Then all the other guests take to the floor.

And Finally

All the single women gather for the bride to toss her bouquet – tradition dictates that whoever catches it will be next to marry. If the couple are not staying at the venue, they can either make their grand exit or slip away to change into going away outfits, before leaving to a first night hotel or the honeymoon.

THE RECEPTION *at home*

TRADITION · MARQUEE · BELLS · GARDENS · FLOWERS · INITIALS · BLUE & WHITE

VANESSA ILBURY AND HUGO ALEXANDER at St Cadoc's church and the groom's family home, South Wales. 'We chose a July wedding because the flowers in the beautiful gardens at The Manor House are at their best during that particular week. The family gardener, who has been with the family for 77 years, delayed his retirement at the age of 91 in order to oversee the wedding.

We chose an English country theme based around ivory and cornflower blue and flowers played an important part in the whole day. The church was decorated with larkspur, White September and lilies with posies at all the pews ends and cascade arrangements of the same flowers at the altar. My bouquet was white Eskimo roses, larkspur, White September and myrtle leaves from the tree in the gardens, echoing the Victorian tradition of using myrtle, which signifies love. Hugo's buttonhole and a rose from my bouquet have since been made into a paperweight memento.

We incorporated the Welsh tradition of giving money to local children as we left the church. Once the children are satisfied with the money have been given, they untie a large ribbon which has been put across the gate allowing the bride and groom to leave.

Our 200 guests were seated in a huge white marquee on the lawns overlooking the sea. We ate a traditional menu of smoked chicken with mango, Welsh beef or Welsh trout and lemon tart piped with our initials in chocolate on the top. The wedding cake was a classic four-tier creation with our entwined initials also forming part of the decoration. The table numbers and menus were handmade by me in the weeks before the wedding.

One of the most memorable moments was hearing The Old Manor's cast iron bell ringing as we arrived for the reception, it had been specially repaired for the wedding and had not rung previously for over 50 years.

Steal their wedding style

- Accommodate guests in a marquee, they come in all shapes and sizes are can fit into a surprisingly small garden
- Incorporate some family traditions into the day, even if it is just getting grandparents or older friends to give the readings
- Nothing shows you care more than a few handmade touches like stationery, table numbers and menus (providing you are suitably artistic!)
- Have boxes of confetti made using your initials
- Theme the flowers around what is growing in the family garden – even using some of these flowers in the bride's bouquet and the groom's buttonhole

'We chose a traditional theme based around beautiful English country garden flowers'

SEASONAL STYLE
and colour

THE WELL CO-ORDINATED wedding will always have a theme of some kind. A harmony of style, colour, and mood ensuring that your celebrations will look and feel right the minute your guests step through the door.

Setting a theme may sound rather grand but it doesn't have to become theatrical, it can be as simple as majoring on one colour or selecting details that suit the season in which you are marrying. Use colour to guide you towards the season for your wedding. If you love rich reds and the flicker of candlelight then a winter wedding is going to suit you perfectly. If pink peonies and strawberries and cream are at the top of your list, anything other than a summer celebration could be disappointment.

Many couples have an image of their wedding from the minute they start planning and you should be guided by this as you progress all the details from the menu to the flowers.

*Colour and texture go a long way towards creating the right mood for any celebration. From classic white roses encased in bold foliage, **above**, to hot pink petals in paper confetti cones, **left**. An artificial flower wreath, **right**, makes the perfect name card holder at a smaller wedding.*

'Marriage is like a
fine wine, as it ages it just
gets *better*'

THE SPRING WEDDING

Spring weddings are all about potential – the earth will be exploding with colour and blossoms and the trick is to bring all that beauty inside your venue for your guests to enjoy.

The Look: Spring colour themes range from bright and sunny to a more subdued pastel palette of pinks, lilac, lemons and creams. Decorate tables with piles of favour boxes in Easter shades of yellow, lilac and blue or treat your guests to individual packets of wildflower seeds which will remind them of your special day long after it is over.

The Dress: In early spring you can still get away with a long-sleeved dress. Otherwise, any style should work, just find the one that suits your figure best. For a real spring feel, go with floral applique or embroidery, or choose butterfly details. If plain white is too predictable, try a dress in a flattering pastel shade. Don't forget to carry a pretty umbrella, just in case.

The Flowers: Choose flowers in soft shapes, such as allium, peonies and sweet peas, and have arrangements in wicker baskets or silver buckets to decorate tables. For a more formal look, go with structured blooms such as lilies, orchids or tulips. A blossom namecard tied to each napkin makes a lovely placecard.

Eat, Drink and Be Married: If you're hosting a cocktail party, serve grown-up hors d'oeuvres and smart cocktails made with fruit juices. Another elegant springtime idea is afternoon tea, complete with piles of pretty fairycakes. For sit-down dinners, supplement your main course with colourful seasonal vegetables. Choose a light pudding, such as white chocolate mousse with fresh berries served in tall glasses drizzled with fresh cream.

Seasonal style tip:

With so many flowers in season, prices will be reasonable so you can afford to indulge in a floral extravaganza. Save on the cake by decorating a plain white iced cake with lots of fresh flowers to match your bouquet.

THE SUMMER WEDDING

For a summer wedding, there's nothing better than country-style wild flowers and simple prints – and the nights should be warm enough for eating *al fresco* on a patio, under a marquee or in a conservatory.

The Look: White is always a cool theme for a summer wedding. Add colour with sheer organza and delicate ribbons in pastel shades that will flutter in the summer sunshine. Candles should be minimal to avoid the illusion of more heat. For afternoons, a white marquee or fashionable Raj-style tent will provide cooling shade, add garlands of flowers for a pastoral theme.

The Dress: To keep your cool, try floaty dress designs in light fabrics such as silk and chiffon. Empire-line styles or a simple sheath look suitably summery and you can invest in a delicate wrap to ward off any evening chill. Make sure your hairstyle won't wilt in the heat.

The Flowers: Ask your florist about flowers that won't droop or shrivel when it's hot. To make a real splash, try sunflowers, or for a more formal look, carry a few white arum lilies tied with satin ribbon. Rethink those enormous flower displays or lighten them with organza and crystal details or fairy lights. For an unusual centrepiece, float flower heads and candles in coloured bowls filled with water.

Eat, Drink and Be Married: Keep hors d'oeuvres light and tasty, avoiding anything that will look 'sweaty' in the heat. Salmon served with salad and new potatoes makes a light main course, strawberries dipped in white chocolate are a good finger-food dessert. Forgo traditional wedding cake in favour of a tower of individual fairy cakes. Lollipops tied with colour ribbon make sweet favours.

Seasonal style tip:

For the most flattering wedding photographs, have them taken in the shade rather than direct sunlight. Sunshine makes you squint and creates dark shadows under your eyes and chin, none of which will make you look your beautiful best. Have a girly parasol to hand to shade your face when you are walking about outside and likely to be snapped by all your guests.

THE AUTUMN WEDDING

Harvest-festival style is not the only option for an autumn wedding. Rich colours such as aubergine, russet and gold work equally well in a contemporary setting.

The Look: The weather should be comfortably cool and the range of decor is almost endless – from opulent to rustic. Candles should play a big part of the decorations, while berries, fruits and even pumpkins can be incorporated in the table arrangements.

The Dress: Many autumn brides choose a dress in a subtle shade of gold, but ivory is also popular and flattering to most type of skin. But be mindful of going too far with a heavy brocade fabric, late September and early October is often warm so plan your outfit with a variety of temperatures in mind. You can always have a warm wrap handy in case you need to cover up.

The Flowers: An autumn bouquet will be brimming with firey, colourful flowers and foliage. Try gerbera, euphorbia, dahlia or yellow calla lilies. Dramatic shower bouquets can include autumnal twigs, berries, herbs and leaves. This is the one season where lots of foliage works well so you can create lots of outsize, and relatively inexpensive, arrangements to stand in doorways and corners.

Eat, Drink and Be Married: Menus can have more intense flavours with hints of ginger and cinnamon. Guests will appreciate warm starters such as stilton tartlets when it's cooler outside. Main courses can be heavier, such as beef or pork loin, with colourful vegetables. Opt for rich desserts such as caramel mousse with raspberry sauce or an indulgent chocolate tart with homemade ice-cream.

Seasonal style tip:

An autumn wedding can be the best of both worlds – neither too hot or too cold. Since the nights are drawing in, make the most of candlelight. Tealights are inexpensive and create an instantly welcoming and romantic atmosphere. They should last four hours without needing to be changed.

THE WINTER WEDDING

Rich jewel shades are a wonderful addition to a winter wedding table. Alternatively, keep everything pure white from the china to the feathers adorning each napkin.

The Look: A traditional winter theme uses sumptuous colours and fabrics and rich gold accents. For a modern alternative, create an ice princess look with your venue filled with white fairy lights and sparkly stars or snowflake decorations. Whatever the colour scheme, remember the days will be short, so add light and atmosphere with twinkling candles - you really can't have too many!

The Dress: For a formal look, choose a long-sleeved dress in a luxurious duchess satin. If you've got your heart set on something more revealing, just cover up with a dramatic cloak or velvet wrap. Winter dresses can't be too opulent – feel free to choose elaborate diamante or crystal beading, intricate embroidery or faux-fur trim.

The Flowers: Opt for deep red velvety roses surrounded by lush greenery, flowing ivy and berries. Grand arrangements work well in winter – they look theatrical and can help breathe life into a gloomy venue. If you're going for a more modern look, carry a simple bouquet of white camellias, amaryllis, orchids, roses or snowdrops. For unusual centrepieces, use colourful Christmas decorations in low bowls.

Eat, Drink and Be Married: Serve mulled wine and filling hors d'oeuvres as guests come in from the cold, then treat them to a hearty feast – everyone always feels hungrier in cold weather. Pumpkin soup makes a delicious starter, followed by roast beef or lamb with traditional vegetables. Finish with a comforting dessert such as treacle tart or sticky toffee pudding.

Seasons and colours

Perfect colour combinations no matter whether you want a traditional or contemporary theme:

SPRING	Pastel pink and white
	Lemon yellow and white
	Gold and ivory
SUMMER	Yellow and mint green
	Cool white
	Tiffany blue and silver
AUTUMN	Orange and russet
	Lilac and lime green
	Gold and cream
WINTER	Ice white
	Silver and white
	Red and rich green

Seasonal style tip:

For the most dramatic effect, choose a rich red theme with accents of green and gold – very Christmassy and seasonal. Or go to the opposite extreme and stick to ice white with touches of clear blue and silver and lots of sparkly decorations. Either way, have fun. This is the one season when more is probably more!

THE WINE COUNTRY *wedding*

ROSES · CHOCOLATE · WHITE FAIRY LIGHTS · CANDLES · CRACKERS · SUNSHINE

SARAH HODGSON AND CHARLES BURTON at The Friendship Trail, Napa Valley, California, USA. 'We chose the venue having visited the Napa Valley on holiday and fell in love with it. Our guests were coming from England (where the bride originally lived) and from all across America so we wanted to create a fun vacation for everyone.

The view across the valley from the estate is breathtaking and with the sunshine we didn't need masses of decoration except candlelight and lots of white fairy lights. I love roses so they played a big part in the day, my bouquet was an arrangement of roses in different shades of white, cream, ivory and a pale blush. We also had pink rose balls hanging from the trees and in the centre of the arbor.

For my 'something old' I wore my grandmother's pearl and diamond necklace, which has been part of the family for over 100 years. She wasn't able to come to the wedding due to illness but I managed to speak to her during the reception, which was a very special moment for me.

The guests feasted on a menu of grilled salmon or filet mignon and drank the local Californian wines. Since I am something of a chocaholic, our cake was very chocolately. The bottom layer was milk chocolate with hazelnut filling (our goal was to have a Nutella cake!), the next layer was Snickers, then a lemon layer and finally a raspberry poundcake as the top tier. We also served warm chocolate chip cookies later in the evening.

I surprised and delighted my husband, who is an Olympic wrestler, with an ice sculpture of the Olympic rings. For favours we had silver wedding crackers filled with Godiva chocolates. It was nice letting our American guests experience a European wedding tradition.

Our magic moment was driving away from the reception in an old Packard convertible. We drove over the mountain and the sky was filled with stars. We sipped champagne and relived the whole amazing day.

Steal their wedding style

- White Christmas lights are inexpensive to buy and brilliant for using as twinkling room divider or as a backdrop for photographs
- Use one flower, like roses, in lots of different shades to bring a sense of continuity and style to the whole day
- Ask your cakemaker to use a variety of flavourings on the different tiers of your cake so you can offer something to suit all tastes
- Ice sculptures can be used as the focal point of any reception. Ice can be moulded into a bar from which to serve sushi or ice cold drinks. It is surprisingly long lasting, even in the summer
- Crackers make fun favours and can be bought empty and filled with mini gifts of your choice

'We fell in love with the venue. The view across the valley from the estate is breathtaking'

CHAPTER 5

WEDDING *flowers*

A WEDDING WOULDN'T be a wedding without gorgeous flowers. And whether your budget is big or small you will want to include some flowers in your celebrations. Your first step towards floral perfection is to find a florist. Flowers set the style for the whole day, so this is an all-important partnership. You are looking for someone in tune with what you like who will bring a sense of style and drama to the whole occasion.

Above A classic arrangement of deliciously scented sweet peas makes a perfect posy for a bridesmaid. *Left* Peonies are one of the most popular wedding flowers and ideal in a traditional bridal bouquet. *Right* A stunning bouquet of roses mixed with wired crystals and beads. Ribbon held together with pearl-tipped pins adds the finishing touch.

'*Falling in love*
is easy, staying in
love requires work'

FINDING YOUR FLORIST

The florist is one of your most important wedding suppliers and you should expect to visit at least three to discuss your ideas. The trick is to find a florist who can make your dreams come true without blowing your budget.

Look through magazines to find florists in the area close to the wedding venue, and ask for recommendations from friends or other suppliers, such as your venue or caterer.

Make appointments with your shortlist of favourites, avoiding Saturday if possible when the shop is bound to be a bit hectic. Arm yourself with details of your wedding (the date, the venue and some idea of what you'd like). It is also important you have some idea of what you want to spend. As a rough estimate, 5% of your total budget is the average.

At this initial meeting, it is also quite usual to take along tearsheets of flowers you like. You won't be expected to know what all of the flowers are called, but pictures do give

Above Tulips are always popular at a spring wedding, simply tied with colour co-ordinated ribbon. *Right* Ask your florist about incorporating tiny fairylights into tablecentres for instant wow factor.

Are you right for my wedding?

When you're visiting potential florists, take along a list of questions to help you decide.

1. Do you have photographs of your work, especially other weddings at my venue?

2. Which flowers will be in season for my wedding?

3. How can I maximize my budget?

4. Do you offer items such as vases and candelabras? Can they be hired or do I need to buy them?

5. Will you personally be doing my flowers? If not, can I meet the florist I will be working with?

6. When do we have to finalize all the flower choices?

7. What would the timetable for the flowers be on the day?

8. Do I need to leave a deposit now and when is the balance due?

the florist a good idea of the type of thing you like as well.

A good florist should be able to come up with designs you love that suit your wedding, while remaining within your budget. If they keep trying to get you to spend more, or want to change your ideas radically, then they are probably not the one for you. On the other hand, don't be disheartened if they try to adapt your ideas. You need to allow them room for creativity, they're the experts after all!

Book your florist anything up to a year in advance of the wedding and expect to pay a deposit at the time you make the booking. Make your initial choices about three months in advance, finalizing all the details about three weeks before the wedding.

STYLE ON A BUDGET

Creating a floral extravaganza with a large budget is easy, but if you don't have a lot to spend, you shouldn't have to compromise on style. Be honest with your florist about your budget, they should be able to keep the costs down without cutting down on quality. Obviously, the easiest way to save money is to have fewer flowers, particularly ornate, time-consuming table arrangements, but there are other ways to save as well.

First of all, be sure to stick to seasonal flowers. Flowers that are out of season will have to be imported or grown in greenhouses so are generally more expensive. If there's a particular flower you really love but it's proving to be expensive, use it sparingly, perhaps only in your bridal bouquet, making it doubly special and even more memorable.

Don't dismiss 'common' flowers either, as they can look stunning. Carnations, for example, can be made up into eyecatching – and inexpensive – pomanders for all your bridesmaids or used as modern centrepieces. Other ways of saving money include using the ceremony flowers at your reception (how about putting your bouquets on the top table?), enhancing larger arrangements with lots of pretty foliage and giving bridesmaids single flowers to carry instead of posies.

Your flowers can also be much more than a visual statement. Surprisingly few blooms need to be used to fill a room with wonderful fragrance. If you want maximum impact ask your florist about using lily of the valley, hyacinth, frangipani, apple blossom, orange blossom, mimosa, stocks, jasmine, sweet peas and snowdrops in some of your arrangements.

Top A simple arrangement of white stocks in an eye-catching mirrored container. *Above* A classic bouquet of perfectly proportioned English garden roses highlighted with wired pearls. *Right* Tumblers packed with delicate campanula look effective when grouped together.

Menu

Chilled assortment of melon, grapes and kiwi fruit marinated in a ginger and sparkling wine syrup

Roasted supreme of chicken finished with a leek, mushroom and garden herb sauce

Assortment of seasonal vegetables and potatoes

COLOUR THEMES AND TRENDS

While the main aim is to choose flowers in a colour that you like, there are other factors to take into consideration. Think about the venues where you will be holding your ceremony and reception. If you love the idea of soft pink flowers but your venue has a scarlet patterned carpet, you might need to rethink your colour scheme. Also, if your venue is modern and minimalist, delicate country flowers in pastel shades will look out of place, whilst striking white lilies would be ideal.

Consider the colours that suit you. If you have a fair complexion and you will be wearing ivory or white, colours such as orange and purple could be overpowering, while cream, pink and white are sure to look pretty.

The simplest solution to setting a theme is to go with the season. Spring and summer demands soft, pastel shades and lots of white. An autumn or winter wedding, when it is likely to be dark, allows you to choose more colour. Reds, splashes of vibrant orange mixed with foliage and lots of candlelight will certainly look dramatic. Ask your florist about incorporating colour in the form of beads, feathers and other fabrics in the table arrangements and your bouquet. This is currently very popular and works particularly well with a contemporary theme.

How many flowers are enough?

Before you speak to your florist it's important to make a list of all the areas in your wedding where you would like to include flowers, and then decide on the designs and styles that will suit each one. Try to visualize the church or ceremony room, reception venue, your bouquet, bridesmaids' flowers, buttonholes and other accessories, writing down the flower requirements for each one so you can chat your ideas through.

If you're having a church wedding, the church may have a florist, or you may decide to use your own. Consider having pedestals at the front of the church and perhaps some flowers at the end of each pew. You might also want to decorate the entrance to the church where many of the photographs will be taken, and provide cones of fresh petals for your guests to throw as confetti.

If you're having a civil ceremony, it is usual to have pedestal or table arrangements where you say your vows. Once this part of the wedding is over, you can move the flowers from the ceremony room into the reception area, instantly halving your flower costs.

The room where the reception is being held is the place to splash out on flowers since it is the place your guests will be spending the most time. First impressions count so the entrance needs to be welcoming, drawing your guests inside. A floral pedestal on either side of the door is ideal or you could frame the door in tulle decorated with a single garland, which looks effective and is inexpensive.

Keep table arrangements either low, no more than 10in high, so that guests can talk over them, or in tall vases so that they can talk under them! Fresh petals can be scattered over tables, arrangements can be tied to the back of chairs, blooms can be suspended in water surrounded by floating candles, and individual flowers can be tied to napkins as favours. Don't feel you have to cover every surface with arrangements. Clever positioning and using displays of varying heights can create a feeling of lots of flowers, even when there are not.

Roses are probably the most popular of all the wedding flowers. There are hundreds of varieties in a myriad of different shades to suit every style of celebration. They look beautiful whether in bud or in full bloom and work for everything from the bouquet to the reception centrepieces.

THE BRIDAL BOUQUET

The bouquet is the ultimate wedding accessory – your options limited only to the availability of the flowers, the skill of the florist and your imagination. The style of your wedding and the shape of your dress will guide you towards the perfect bouquet.

Getting the balance between your outfit and the flowers means that you shouldn't finalize your flowers until after you have chosen your dress. A large bouquet, for example, could overpower a simple, straight or slinky dress, while a small, delicate posy will be drowned by a dramatic, full-skirted gown and traditional accessories. To perfect this, you should always take a picture or sketch of your dress to your florist so that he or she can bear the shape in mind when creating your bouquet. You might also like to think about having matching fresh flowers made to wear in your hair.

Keeping your bouquet looking fresh can be a worry, especially in hot weather. Try to handle it as little as possible once it arrives, leaving it nestled in tissue paper and out of direct sunlight until the last minute. Contrary to popular belief, you should not put it in the fridge, flowers do not like any extremes of temperature. Just as you are about to leave, pinch out any bruised leaves and fluff the edges which may have been flattened in transit. Always hold your bouquet away from your body to prevent crushing the flowers and marking your dress. If you want to keep your bouquet after the wedding, get your florist to make a smaller version to use for the bridal flower toss. Ask your mum to take your bouquet home after the wedding and hang it in a dark airing cupboard for a couple of weeks prior to preservation.

Hand-tied posies are the most popular style of bridal bouquet. They suit all shapes of wedding dress and are easy to hold. Ask your florist to choose colour co-ordinated and luxurious ribbon to tie around the stems, perhaps fastening with coloured beads or wired pearls.

Styles of bridal bouquet

Posy: small, simple and usually hand-tied with ribbon. Lily of the valley makes the perfect minimalist posy.

Round: the classic bouquet, usually consisting of larger flowers such as roses and peonies that are loosely arranged.

Hand-tied: blooms that are wired together or casually hand-tied. Works best in an informal setting with a modern, slinky dress.

Shower: a waterfall-like spill of flowers wired to cascade from the bride's hands. Petite brides or anyone wearing a very simple dress should be wary of this style, since it is a potentially overwhelming bouquet. This is the most traditional and formal of all the bouquets.

MAIDS AND BUTTONHOLES

Bridesmaids' flowers should echo the style and colour of your bouquet. The most popular option is to give each maid an identical posy. Or you could let each maid carry her favourite flower so you have different flowers, but all in the same colour. A single, long-stemmed flower such as a lily is currently very fashionable at contemporary weddings.

Younger flowergirls often enjoy carrying a small bag filled with flowers or fresh petals to scatter over the floor. If you don't want them to have to carry anything, ask your florist to design pretty hair decorations. For tiny maids, a teddy bear wearing a fresh corsage is a sweet alternative and doubles as a thank-you gift.

Buttonholes always look smart on a dark suit and help to tie the whole wedding party together. Your groom will probably like to have something different from his best man and ushers – ideally a flower taken from your bouquet. It's also a lovely idea to give fathers a buttonhole and both mothers a pretty corsage to pin on their jackets or handbag.

Below *The groom's buttonhole should ideally be the same flower as one from the bride's bouquet.* **Right** *All bridesmaids, big and small, look pretty with wired flowers in their hair and a small posy to carry.*

The meaning of flowers

Incorporate one of the more romantic flowers into your theme and send a secret message of love to your groom.

Arum lily	ardour
Azalea	true to the end
Carnation (red)	admiration
Carnation (white)	sweet and lovely
Daffodil (yellow)	joy
Daisy	innocence
Forget-me-not	true love
Freesia	sweetness
Geranium	true friendship
Gerbera	cheerfulness
Hibiscus	delicate beauty
Honeysuckle	bonds of love
Hyacinth	playfulness
Iris	hope and wisdom
Jasmine	sensuality
Lemon blossom	fidelity
Lily (white)	youth and beauty
Lily of the valley	happiness
Mallow	consumed by love
Mimosa	sensitivity
Orchid	magnificent/beauty
Ranunculus	you are attractive
Rose (pink)	happiness
Rose (red)	I love you
Rose (yellow)	friendship
Rose (white)	purity
Snowdrop	hope
Sunflower	adoration
Sweet pea	lasting pleasures
Tulip (red)	love
Tulip (yellow)	sunshine of my life
Violet	faithfulness

Help to make the most of your budget and keep costs down by choosing flowers that are in season for your wedding.

Spring

Amaryllis: A large open flower in colours from white to bright red. Perfect for larger bouquets and centrepieces.

Anemone: Available in about 120 varieties. The brighter colours are great for trendy posies.

Daffodil: A bright yellow flower that is always popular for spring weddings.

Freesia: Small, highly scented flowers in bright colours. Ideal for headdresses and posies.

Gerbera: Large and dramatic, daisy-like flowers that come in orange, red, yellow and pink.

Lily of the valley: Tiny, bell-shaped white flowers with a sweet fragrance, ideal for small posies.

Orchid: Exotic and pricey but available in a variety of pretty colours. Just a few long stems simply tied make a stunning modern bouquet.

Ranunculus: A buttercup-like flower popular for spring weddings. Available in a variety of colours.

Stephanotis: A traditional and popular white wedding flower with a wonderful scent.

Sweet pea: A classic wedding favourite with delicate petals and a sweet, lingering scent.

Work with your florist to discover which flowers will be in season at the time of your wedding. There should be something special to suit your colour scheme at any time of the year. If you have one particular favourite flower that is not in season, and therefore more expensive, keep this just for your bouquet and the groom's buttonhole.

Summer

Anthurium: Famous for its glossy, waxy-looking flowers. Popular for beach and tropical themes.

Carnation: The traditional choice for a buttonhole. Also works well en-masse in pomanders for bridesmaids. Available in lots of colours.

Gypsophilia: Tiny white or pink flowers that form a cloud-like display. Best used en masse.

Lily: There are about 100 varieties in a range of colours from white to brilliant red. Ideal for bouquets or reception tablecentres.

Magnolia: Large, subtly scented flowers in a wide range of shapes and colours. Popular for reception decorations.

Peony: Large, fragrant flowers with petals in a bowl shape. Make a wonderfully modern bouquet in pale pink or white.

Rose: The most popular of all wedding flowers and used for bouquets and decorations. Available in a huge variety of shapes and colours.

Sunflower: A refreshing choice for a summer wedding. They can be expensive but they are so large you won't need many.

Autumn

Agapanthus: Large, bell-shaped heads in a striking violet-blue. Adds a splash of colour to bouquets and centrepieces.

Aster: Small, daisy-like flowers in a wide variety of colours, usually with a bright yellow centre. Pretty in all sorts of bouquets.

Clematis: Perfect for trailing bouquets, available in a wide range of flower sizes and colours.

Daisy: A year-round favourite which always looks bright and cheerful. The ideal flower on which to theme your wedding.

Hosta: Not strictly a flower but a variety of popular foliage with heart-shaped leaves. Ranging in colour from a soft blue to bright green.

Hydrangea: Large, full flowers in a variety of pretty pastel colours. Good for centrepieces and pedestal arrangements.

Passion flower: Large exotic flowers that can be used to add splashes of bright colour.

Pinks: Not surprisingly, available in a variety of shades of pinks, from pale to almost red. Pretty round flowers, ideal for bouquets.

Winter

Camellia: Glorious open-faced flowers ranging from a single row of petals to overlapping multi-rows. Popular for button-holes because of the foliage.

Euphorbia: An evergreen shrub with yellowish-green flowers. Useful as a year-round addition to venue arrangements and more elaborate bouquets.

Heather: A lovely rich lilac coloured flower to incorporate into winter table arrangements.

Iris: An unusual fan-shaped flower with three large petals. Usually white, lilac or purple and popular for centrepieces.

Nerine: Sprays of hot or pale pink trumpet-shaped flowers. Quite exotic so good for unusual centrepieces.

Pansy: Small, flat-faced flowers in a variety of colours from pale to bright. Best for adding vibrant colours to reception flowers.

Snowdrop: A delicate, pure white flower and one of the classic bridal flowers. Ideal in hand-tied posies and for smaller table decorations.

Tulip: A favourite available in a wide variety of colours. The variety with frilled edges are popular for modern bouquets.

THE AMERICAN RANCH *wedding*

RANCH SETTING · SUNSHINE · BRIGHT COLOURS · SUNFLOWERS · NATURE

JEN KINAVEY AND SEAN RIEBLI at The Atwood Ranch, Glen Ellen, California, USA. 'We nearly didn't get married at all since our wedding was scheduled for September 14th 2001, just three days after the nightmare of September 11th. We were filled with doubts about whether we, and our guests, would be in the mood for celebration and to go ahead with the wedding was one of the hardest decisions we'll ever make. As it turned out it was probably the best day of our lives. Many guests thanked us for holding the wedding since it was just what people needed - to be surrounded by the love and friendship of family and friends.

We chose the venue because it captures the essence of historic Sonoma; a vineyard, rolling California hills and ranch living. We thought the barn would be the perfect place to party after the dinner on the lawns next to the vineyard.

I am very fortunate to have Sonoma's premier florist, Anne Appleman, as my sister-in-law. I asked her to use a theme of bright, fun colours and she did the rest. She chose many flowers (and lots of citrus fruits) but the main ones were sunflowers and gerberas in shades of pink and the most brilliant orange. We covered jam jars in gingham fabric and used these as candle holders dotted throughout the barn. They helped to create a barn dance quality which encouraged everyone to let their hair down and dance the night away.

Sean comes from a ranching family so an all-American menu suited everyone perfectly. Guests had a choice of filet mignon or roasted chicken. Appetizers were California oysters and prawn cocktail. Once seated, guests were served with a mixture of salads, local artisan breads, various cheeses and piles of fresh fruits. The whole meal had a relaxed family-style quality that was important to us.

One of my memorable moments was a CD we had burned of all our favourite records which we gave to each guest as a favour. It included *The Way You Look Tonight*, *Makin' Whoopie*, *You Are My Sunshine* and *L-O-V-E*. The playlist appealed to all ages and was a huge success.

Steal their wedding style

- Use jam jars tied with ribbon as candleholders. They are inexpensive, look great and are safe even with little children around
- Citrus fruits like oranges, limes and lemons sliced and used to line bowls and jugs bring a splash of colour to any table centre
- A barn dance is guaranteed to appeal to guests of all ages, it's informal and lots of fun
- A barbeque is perfect for an outdoor wedding, meat and fish served with lots of interesting salad
- Sunflowers and gerberas are excellent wedding flowers. Big and bright and they last well even in the heat

'The barn dance encouraged everyone to let their hair down and dance the night away'

CHAPTER 6

WEDDING *details*

Yᴏᴜ'ᴠᴇ ᴄʜᴏsᴇɴ ʏᴏᴜʀ dress, booked the venues, organized the entertainment and now it is time to have some fun! Once all the major decisions are made you can concentrate on all those lovely little details that will stamp your personal style on the day. And you know what? In my experience, it is often these little details that your friends and family remember most fondly rather than the grandness of the venue, the weather and what was on the menu.

Above *You don't need to make extravagant gestures, a simple napkin, name card and a single flower will always look classy.* **Left** *Napkins always look stylish when tied with a piece of ribbon which can be finished to suit your theme with anything from flowers to feathers.* **Right** *For a dramatic splash of colour at each place setting, add a pile of flower heads or use petal confetti which can later be scattered over the table as extra decoration.*

'The *more you invest* in a marriage, the *more valuable* it becomes'

LIGHTING AND ATMOSPHERE

You should never underestimate the importance of lighting for creating the right atmosphere. Speak to the lighting specialist at your venue who can advise you on what is achieveable in the rooms you have chosen.

Fluorescent lighting should be banned from your wedding. Even in winter gloom the effect is too harsh and more suited to a conference than a celebration. Most large venues will have dimmer switches on their lights or bulbs can be replaced with lower wattages for a softer effect.

Think about angling spotlights to accent a spectacular floral arrangement in a corner or to highlight the wedding cake table. Fairylights are inexpensive and can be draped over mantlepieces and up staircases. Curtains of tiny white lights from a garden centre look beautiful hung across a plain wall. They can also be used as a subtle room divider, perhaps curtaining off a dance area and look lovely in photographs.

If your guests will be going outside onto a patio or into gardens, flaming torches are an effective and welcoming way of lining pathways and illuminating trees.

Candles are my favourite way of creating a romantic atmosphere and I would suggest any bride having a wedding after five o'clock to scatter them liberally across every surface she can. Tealights in simple glass votives are invaluable. They are very cheap to buy in bulk and are pretty safe for your guests, even younger members of the wedding party. Use them plain or try a little DIY decoration. You don't have to be an artist to tie a strip of organza ribbon around each one or spray them with paint for great effect.

Candles can be incorporated into your tablecentres too. Ask your florist about using a mixture of short and tall candlesticks as part of the arrangements. Most florists have a range of candles and candlesticks that you can hire. Stick to white/cream candles though, even if you are having a strong colour theme as coloured candles never look stylish.

Candlelight is a must at just about every wedding. It adds instant romance to any venue and softens the atmosphere in the most boring of function rooms. Buy inexpensive votives in bulk and sticker with your wedding date. Or splash out and hire larger candles and more elaborate holders from your florist which can be incorporated in your tablecentres.

TAKE YOUR PLACES

Your guests will be spending up to three hours sitting at the reception table, so you want each place setting to look the part. My advice is always to stick to good quality white linens, white china and silver cutlery with crystal stemware. You can personalize the table with the details you add.

Rather than numbering each table – which can cause offence to those guests on tables with high numbers – name the tables after flowers or places that have a special meaning for the happy couple. Make sure the name is positioned high enough that guests can easily spot their designated table from across the room.

Invest in at least two seating plans, three if you are having a large number of guests, printing them large enough so that they can be viewed easily. Many stationers will print seating plans to match the rest of your stationery, alternatively print it yourself on a computer and blow it up to A1 size on a photocopier. Borrow several easels and position on either side of the door leading into the reception.

Welcome your guests to the table with a place card showing their name. The most formal card is simply scripted but you can have some fun by affixing a tiny silk flower onto each one with a dab of glue. Alternatively, punch a hole across the top of each card and thread with a colourful strip of thin ribbon. Large leaves can double as place cards, use a metallic silver or gold to write each name. Another idea is to spray a pear with gold paint and then attach a small name card to the stalk with fine ribbon.

Tie napkins in a variety of creative ways using coloured ribbons or beaded cord in a bow or simple loop, tucking a flower stem, dramatic leaf or a curl of ivy into each one.

Menu cards are usually placed onto each plate, outlining in delicious detail the feast that is to come. It is also quite acceptable to position one menu card between two places or even to place a single menu card in the centre of the table.

Your guests will be spending several hours sitting at the reception so welcome them with a stylish table plan and then pretty details like place names and table numbers that match your theme.

FANTASTIC FAVOURS

Favours or little gifts for each guest have become very much part of the modern wedding. The traditional favour comprises five sugared almonds tied in a fabric bag and secured with ribbon and perhaps a little tag highlighting their meaning; health, wealth, happiness, fertility and long life. But there are lots of other ideas for favours including miniature bottles of alcohol with labels printed with the wedding date, packets of seeds, lottery tickets, teddy bears, individual chocolates, tiny picture frames, soaps, sachets of herbs and even tiny jars of marmalade. Many couples choose different favours for male and female guests, adding extra colour and variety to their table.

PLEASE BE SEATED

The chairs in most venues are pretty standard, usually gold or plain wood with a red, gold or silver cushion pad – and these are ripe for decoration. Slipcovers are the most popular option and a must if the chairs are not in good condition, but they can be expensive if you are having a large wedding. Your venue or a hire company will be able to provide them in a variety of fabrics and with a large number of colour co-ordinating bows. If you are on a budget you could just cover the chairs of the bride and groom.

Another way to decorate reception chairs is to ask the stationery company to make 6-inch square name cards which can be threaded with colourful ribbon and tied onto each chair.

Favours Tiny gifts welcoming each guest to the table is a nice touch. Choose just about anything you like from traditional sugared almonds in a box to individual chocolates. **Chairbacks** Decorating the backs of chairs looks fantastic but can be expensive. If you are on a budget, just decorate the chairs of the happy couple.

ENTERTAINING IDEAS

Once the last crumbs of cake have been eaten your guests will want to get into the party mood. Reception entertainment needs to suit the style and formality of the wedding. A five-piece band is perfect for a smart evening reception in a hotel, whereas a good DJ with a deck is suitable for more informal surroundings like a marquee. If your budget allows, you may want to mix the entertainment as the evening progresses, starting with a trio singing popular ballards moving on to a disco as the drinks start to flow.

Think about other types of entertainment too. Magicians moving around the tables while your guests are eating, a silhouette artist, celebrity lookalikes and face painters or even a clown for smaller guests will all help to get the party swinging. A more formal wedding may benefit from the services of a toastmaster. He will set the right tone and ensure that everything ticks along according to plan.

Entertaining ideas for every wedding ...

An afternoon drinks reception for 50 guests

SUGGESTIONS: A quality singer or group of singers able to perform a variety of popular ballards from Sinatra to Robbie Williams. A close-up magician who can move around your guests performing a variety of tricks to groups of three or four people.

A reception with lots of children

SUGGESTIONS: A creche in a separate room is always a good idea, especially if you are inviting large numbers of children under-six. These should be staffed by qualified childminders who will provide a variety of activities like colouring, board games and puzzles for most ages up to about ten years old. Older children will probably enjoy being seated on an adult-free table of their own during the reception, perhaps with a special kiddie-friendly menu and colouring pens and paper to keep them occupied.

A wedding weekend with 100 guests

SUGGESTIONS: A welcoming cocktail party with celebrity lookalikes. They're a great ice-breaker and will get everyone in the party mood as they try to work out whether or not you have invited the real thing. At the end of the wedding reception finish with a spectacular firework display, including the happy couple's initials encased in a heart of fire. Revive jaded guests the day after the wedding with a barbeque serving themed buffets with an Oriental, Middle Eastern and South American flavour. If the weather permits, you could also organize a game of cricket or a football match between the groom's friends and the bride's friends.

A formal reception with 200 guests

SUGGESTIONS: Entertain guests with a classic five-piece band playing traditional jazz tunes. They will be loud enough for everyone to hear, play music the majority will love and are perfect for either listening or dancing to. Later in the evening, set up a casino, real money doesn't change hands but specialist companies can provide all the equipment including roulette wheels, chips and the staff.

An intimate reception with less than 50 guests

SUGGESTIONS: A string quartet or a smooth jazz rhythm and blues trio with a laid-back, easy listening style that is not too intrusive. A charicaturist or silhouette cutter can manage this number of guests easily so that everyone will be captured on paper before the party has ended.

10 tips to keep your guests smiling

1. Guests who receive an invitation three weeks before the wedding assume – probably correctly – that they're not on the A-list. If you're planning to send additional invites as cancellations come in, push back the entire process by a month or so, ensuring all guests feel welcome.

2. Include a map with your invitations or your guests may arrive late and grumpy. It's also nice to include a letter detailing local hotel and transport details.

3. Give close friends a ring to ask who they'll be bringing so you can write relevant names on the invitations rather than 'And Guest' which is rather impersonal.

4. Set up a wedding website so guests are up to date with details such as venue information, directions, places to stay, even gift registry information. After the event, you can post photographs for friends and family who couldn't make it on the day.

5. While you're having your photographs taken, which can take an hour or so, make sure your guests have something to drink, nibbles and some entertainment.

6. Don't keep your guests in the dark about what's happening throughout the day. Print timings such as ceremony, drinks reception, sit-down, dancing and departure onto the invitation.

7. Sitting with a lot of strangers is never much fun. If your seating plan is causing huge headaches, think about having a buffet instead and everyone can seat themselves.

8. Plan the dance music carefully otherwise you could have an empty dance floor. Provide a 'quiet room' if possible for older guests to sit and chat.

9. For evening guests, try to provide something more than soggy sandwiches to welcome them to your celebrations. Even if a cash bar has been started, evening guests should be greeted with a complimentary cocktail.

10. Many guests still believe they cannot leave until the newlyweds have departed. If the two of you intend to dance into the night, make sure the DJ announces this news early on letting everyone know they can leave whenever they like.

Borrow a tradition from another country

Give yourselves the luck of the IRISH by putting lavender in your bouquet. It's supposed to bring good fortune and make all your wishes come true.

Stroll down an evergreen-decorated path like GERMAN and DUTCH couples do. The greens represent constancy – perfect for the wedding day.

Candles can be used to symbolize new beginnings and the joining together to two families. In the USA, couples often include a unity candle ceremony. The bride's parents light one candle and the groom's parents light another. After taking the vows, the bride and groom each light a taper from the respective family's candle and meet in front of the unity candle which is then lit together.

Mehndi or henna has great significance at EASTERN celebrations, and no wedding is complete without the decoration of the bride's hands and feet. The mehndi night is a bit like a hen night, with the bride's female friends and relatives gathering to celebrate by singing traditional songs. The groom's name is often hidden in the design, and it can be quite a challenge to find it.

The VICTORIAN tradition of something old, new, borrowed and blue is a popular tradition borrowed by modern brides. Something old symbolizes the stability of marriage and shows you are not forgetting your heritage. Something new represents the new adventure you are embarking on as a married woman. Something borrowed symbolizes the love and support of family and friends as you borrow an item from a happily married woman. Blue traditionally represents love and fidelity.

Bomboniere or favours for your guests have long been a tradition in ITALY. The typical favour is five sugared almonds tied together in a pouch. These symbolize the sweet (sugar) and bitter (almond) aspects of life and the five represent health, wealth, fertility, happiness and longevity.

Ringing bells is a tradition in EASTERN and CHRISTIAN cultures, signifying communication with the spirits. Ringing church bells at the end of a wedding is a joyous public declaration of the marriage. Incorporate bell ringing into your service by handing out tiny hand bells to each of your guests to ring as you and your new husband walk up the aisle after the ceremony.

Incorporating a tradition from another country is an effective way of tying together two cultures, perhaps representing the families of the bride and groom. The most popular tradition is the five sugared almonds used as a wedding favour and borrowed from Italy, where this has been popular for hundreds of years.

THE LONG WEEKEND *wedding*

MODERN · SOPHISTICATED · ORIENTAL LANTERNS · FLOWERS · CANDLES

SYLENA GOODMAN AND MICHAEL LYONS at Beaulieu Vineyard, Rutherford, California, USA. We wanted a beautiful, romantic, outdoor wedding – small enough that everyone could meet each other and it would feel intimate. We also wanted more of a wedding weekend starting with a wine tasting and outdoor buffet on Friday which gave everyone the chance to relax and get to know one another.

I carried a bouquet of white cabbage roses tied with an amazing wide periwinkle blue ribbon. The bridesmaids each carried a different coloured posy in shades of peach, yellow and pink. The groom and ushers all wore buttonholes made from stephanotis flowers. We put a large bowl of the same flowers at the ceremony, complete with pins so that all the men could wear one and the ladies could put one in their hair.

Mike's parents walked him down the aisle and my parents walked me down the aisle, a lovely moment bringing the two families together.

We started the meal with a cocktail hour offering guests a selection of martinis – apple, chocolate, classic martini, cosmopolitans and lemon drop – which were a big hit. Our guests then feasted on a starter of mushrooms, roasted artichoke hearts, leeks and peppers with a main course of delicious crusted Chilean sea bass. The wedding cake was a double chocolate creation in a white fondant shell based on the fabric of my dress with replica sugar rosebuds from my gown scattered over the top.

The centrepieces on each table at the reception were large handblown bowls filled with water-floating candles, gardenias, stephanotis, blue hydrangea and delphinium blossom. There was a ring of votives around each bowl. Each napkin was secured with an individual flower blossom. The venue also had a swimming pool which we surrounded with organza bags containing white candles.

As a fitting end to the day, all our guests were given sparklers and we left in a shower of light before flying off to Hong Kong and Bali on our honeymoon.

Steal their wedding style

- Cocktails are popular way to welcome guests to any wedding, instantly creating a contemporary and stylish start to the party
- Choose a wedding cake to double as the dessert, or have tiers of the cake made from different flavours. Keep the fruit top tier and serve the other 2–3 tiers as dessert with a fruit coulis or homemade ice-cream
- Floating flower heads or candles in a bowl of water makes a beautiful and inexpensive tablecentre
- Choose one main theme colour – in this case periwinkle blue – and introduce it into the flowers, the bridesmaids outfits, the tablecentres and the food tables to bring a sense of harmony to the whole day

'We wanted a beautiful wedding, small enough that everyone could get to know one another'

CHAPTER 7

THE WEDDING
menu

THE FOOD IS one of the most memorable parts of any wedding reception. Think of the menu as a theatrical production with a tantalizing start, a substantial middle and a surprising ending that leaves everyone wanting just a little bit more. Work with your caterers to combine interesting flavours with dishes that look appetising on the plate and a selection of well matched wines that will complement each course.

The food and drink will take up the biggest slice of your wedding budget so you want to get maximum taste as well as great presentation for your money. Ask potential caterers for sample menus to suit the time of year, the formality of your wedding and your budget. You should expect to be offered several alternatives, including something interesting for your vegetarian guests.

Once you have chosen a caterer, arrange a tasting session where you can see and eat what they are suggesting. The wines to accompany the dishes should also be available to sample. Don't be afraid to suggest changes, your caterers are professionals and if you feel that a particular dish will not appeal to your guests, for whatever reason, then say so.

A printed menu card in the style of all your other stationery is a nice idea to welcome your guests to the table and to tempt their tastebuds with a list of the mouthwatering dishes that are to come.

Tim & Fiona's Wedding

Saturday July 13th 2002

Scallop Ravioli, Pernod Cream
~
Farm House Chicken Terrine
~
Rump of Lamb, Confit Fennel & Thyme Jus
~
Hazelnut Brownie with Peanut Butter Ice Cream
~
Coffee & Petit Fours

WINES
Veuve Clicquot Ponsardin

La Princesse Sancerre 2001
Rouge Homme Cabernet Merlot 1996
Chateau Canset de La Tour Saint
Emillion Grand cru 1996

'Life *without love*
is like a tree without
blossom and *fruit*'

LEVELS OF FORMALITY

The most formal and traditional style of wedding reception is a cocktail hour followed by a sit down meal. Welcome drinks can be a glass of champagne, a sparkling wine cocktail, mulled wine in winter or a fruit punch in the summer plus lots of non-alchoholic alternatives like fruit juices and flavoured water. Your guests will also appreciate a selection of canapés, particularly if the meal is still some time away.

A sit-down meal, usually three or four courses, served by waiting staff can be presented at any time from lunchtime onwards but is usually served between 5–7pm depending on the timing of the ceremony.

A buffet is often suggested as the budget alternative to a sit-down meal but this is often not the case. Buffets still need tables and chairs, staff to serve the dishes and to clear it all away. You will also have to have at least two food stations to avoid long queues, more if you are having a large number of guests, and you will be offering more food choices which can quickly add up. Wedding buffets are most successful when you want to create a less formal atmosphere.

For a smaller wedding you may like to think about an early afternoon brunch with dishes like scrambled eggs and smoked salmon, bagels and cream cheese and eggs benedict all washed down with lashing of Bloody Marys, mimosas (peach juice and champagne) and a medley of fruit juices. Afternoon tea presents a wonderful opportunity to serve delicate sandwiches with a variety of fillings, scones and cream and piles of decorated fairy cakes.

If you have guests being invited to the evening proceedings only, they will still expect to be fed. A buffet of cold meats, fish dishes, goats cheese tartlets, salads, interesting breads, cheese, fruit and perhaps a chocolate and strawberry mousse are perfect and will probably be enjoyed by some of the day guests if they are feeling peckish as the dancing starts.

I went to a wedding recently where the couple led the dancing until well after midnight when a late supper (or maybe an early breakfast) of mini hot dogs, kedgeree, scrambled eggs and pots of freshly brewed coffee were most welcome at 2am.

Whatever style of meal you decide on, make it clear on the invitations what will be happening and when you expect the day to finish. There's nothing worse than guests expecting to party on into the evening, when you were ending everything after your stylish tea party.

Left For a memorable centrepiece to a buffet table, ask your caterer or an ice specialist about an ice sculpture. These amazing creations can be made in the shape of a swan, fish or flowers and last a surprisingly long time, even in the middle of the summer. ***Right*** A wedding is a huge celebration so acknowledge the fact with a banner attached to the reception gate or at the doorway with the couple's names and the wedding date and perhaps a huge 'Wedding Congratulations.' At a more formal wedding, use a pair of flags with the couple's initials entwined on them positioned so that all the guests can see them.

YOUR CATERING BUDGET

What you spend on food and drink at the reception takes the largest slice of the wedding budget for many couples. To work out how much you are likely to spend, and whether this suits your proposed budget, try this simple formula.

Most catering companies and hotels charge per head so split the approximate amount you want to spend on food by the number of guests you are inviting. Then you can sit down with the various packages offered by the caterers to see if you can afford to feed your guests for the amount per head you have allocated. It is amazing how quickly a wedding reception menu can add up, so be realistic from the outset rather than setting your heart on some elaborate meal that you cannot really afford. If your budget does seem a bit tight, speak to the caterers to see where they can suggest making effective savings – it could be as simple as changing from meat to fish.

Complete this checklist of what you envisage for quick reference when talking to caterers.

Style of proposed meal
❐ Brunch
❐ Lunch
❐ Afternoon tea
❐ Cocktail party
❐ Dinner
❐ Additional food for evening-only guests

Style of service
❐ Cocktails
❐ Served canapés
❐ Hors d'oeuvres tables
❐ Seated meal
❐ Staff served buffet
❐ Self-service buffet
❐ Food stations

Menu options
❐ Continental
❐ Regional
❐ Seasonal
❐ Exotic
❐ Vegetarian

❐ Ethnic
❐ Themed

Entrées
❐ Beef
❐ Chicken
❐ Vegetarian
❐ Pork
❐ Lamb
❐ Seafood
❐ Pasta

Dessert options
❐ Cake only
❐ Additional desserts

Alcohol options
❐ Full bar
❐ Cash bar
❐ Limited bar (open certain hours only)
❐ Wine with meal
❐ Champagne toast
❐ Cocktails

TEMPTING SEASONAL MENUS

To tempt your tastebuds and give you an idea of the types of dishes that will be suggested to you by your caterers, here are a selection of favourite dishes to suit every style of wedding.

Classic Winter Menu

A wonderful combination of fresh, seasonal produce. The pudding speaks for itself, rich, sinful comfort food – an essential on a winter's day and your guests will love it!

- STARTER
  Gateau of hot smoked salmon with avocado salsa, winter leaves, herb oil and balsamic syrup
- MAIN COURSE
  Roast duck breast, celeriac purée, roast root vegetables, lentil and tarragon sauce
- PUDDING
  Hot ginger treacle pudding, vanilla ice cream and toffee sauce

Classic Summer Menu

A cool summer combination that is light yet substantial. The flavours, such as handmade sausages and salmon with cucumber and strawberries, will titillate your guests palates.

- STARTER
  Medallions of English-style pork sausages with apple chutney on a bed of leaves
- MAIN COURSE
  Fresh salmon garnished and served with cucumber and strawberries and a black pepper crème fraiche, new potatoes, salad of mixed leaves and cherry tomatoes with lime
- PUDDING
  Pear and nut tartlet with Armagnac cream

Vegetarian Menu

This menu looks pretty and has some luxury items in it that make it special. It is also a hot meal, which is good for a winter wedding. Non-vegetarians will be happy since the dishes are filling and have plenty of flavour.

- STARTER
  Warm artichoke hearts stuffed with wild mushrooms served on a bed of green leaves, homemade bread and butter
- MAIN COURSE
  Individual grilled aubergine and red pepper tarts with goat's cheese served with roasted plum tomato sauce and small leek and potato cakes
- PUDDING
  Hazelnut meringues with chocolate cream and chocolate curls

Summer Buffet

Nothing beats an English summer and the food on this menu has been selected to complement a perfect late summer evening. It has a rustic quality that would make if perfect for a wedding in the country.

- BUFFET
  Whole smoked English glazed ham with Cumberland sauce, onion marmalade, pickled cucumbers and onions.

Never feel embarrassed about asking your catering company or the reception venue for a tasting session. However good the menu suggestions the only way to know whether it is to your taste is to try it. Ideally, you should be able to sample the dishes alongside the suggested wines to see whether the flavours all work together.

served with fresh baked soda bread.

Seafood platters of fennel and cod with brown shrimps

Razor clam and potato salad

Brown shrimp with cucumber vinaigrette

Pea purée with seared king scallops

Oysters with shallot vinegar, lemons and black pepper

Rabbit and wood pigeon pie

Game and foie gras terrine

Whole stilton with port

Leeks vinaigrette

Quail's eggs with celery salt

Grilled potatoes, flat field mushrooms and Jerusalem artichokes

- **PUDDING**

  Shot glasses of gooseberry fool

  White chocolate and chestnut cheesecake

  Bowls of plums and damsons

Winter Buffet

This Victorian-style feast combines wonderful rich reds and purples and the generous flavours of traditional British food, creating a warm theme for a chilly night.

- **BUFFET**

  Canapés

  Potted stilton with walnuts and oatcakes

  Jugged kipper and horseradish

  Kedgeree

  Game pie with potato and parsnip pastry

  Roast salmon with mustard butter

  Blue cheese and pear tart

  Braised red cabbage with caraway and juniper

  Brussels sprouts with chestnuts

- **PUDDING**

  Orange and ginger pudding

  Rich chocolate and violet truffle

Budget Menu

A delicious combination that your guests will never imagine is a budget option. This menu can be served silver-service or as a fork buffet, depending on whether you pay extra for waiting staff.

- **STARTER**

  Pâté with blackberries or tomato and mozzarella salad

- **MAIN COURSE**

  Lamb cutlets or beef paupiettes with
  stuffed tomato and petits pois

- **PUDDING**

  Sticky toffee pudding
  or poached pear with chocolate sauce

TASTE SENSATIONS

When it comes to menus, table decorations and drinks who better to ask than the experts? Two of my favourite event organizers set out the essential elements for the coolest wedding reception.

Johnny Roxburgh, The Admirable Crichton

The key to getting the food right for your wedding reception is to keep it simple but use the finest ingredients. It's better to have a large portion of salmon or best-quality pasta than a tiny amount of lobster. Delicious fresh ingredients carefully prepared are far better than something sitting in a coulis or an ocean of jus.

Menus should be themed to the season, so a summer wedding will focus on light ingredients such as fish and plenty of fresh fruit. When planning canapés, allow about 12 per person and make sure they complement the drinks you have chosen.

Champagne is the classic wedding drink so try to serve the best you can afford. Otherwise, opt for a good sparkling wine mixed with framboise liqueur. Interesting cocktails are a good alternative to champagne, just keep the alcohol content low – alcohol is like rocket fuel on an empty stomach! And make sure the soft drinks are interesting, too. It's a good idea to have different glasses for different drinks so staff know who is drinking what when they're topping up.

When it comes to presentation, every item of food should be given the same attention as the wedding dress. Innovative canapé trays, maybe scattered with rose petals, and carefully thought out table displays and tableware will enhance the food. Keep cutlery, crystal and tableware simple and always use large glasses. Be sure not to overcrowd tables, as guests need to be able to speak to each other easily.

Presentation is all-important at any wedding reception. Ask to see how your caterer is proposing to serve the various dishes you have chosen. If necessary you may want to hire more interesting plates and glasses so that the food looks as good as it tastes.

Fiona Dalrymple, Delectable Feasts

Each couple is different and their personalities should show through in the wedding arrangements and reception to make their day distinctive. We like to keep things simple – soft, elegant pastel or cream shades with hints of colour.

If you have a lot of guests, stick to a menu that will suit all age groups. For a traditional wedding, everyone loves champagne for a celebration. On a shoestring, you can always offer an inexpensive sparkling wine served with a hint of framboise. As a non-alcoholic alternative, try serving lime and lemon grass cordial with mint ice cubes.

When it comes to starters, use bright under plates. A colourful starter of saffron risotto with smoked halibut, rocket, baby broad beans and sunkissed tomatoes looks fabulous on a lime green plate. For vegetarians we always suggest serving the same as everyone else but, for example, replacing the fish with a little cheese. The main course should be something such as roasted quail with roasted red onions, marinated in homemade damson vinegar. Chocolate espresso cups are a satisfying finish – deep and smooth.

For a trendy wedding on a budget, I would recommend fun cocktails at a stand-up drinks reception, along with champagne and a soft passion fruit sparkling cordial. Substantial canapés are just the thing – goat's cheese soufflés in mini terracotta pots, little metal buckets full of fish and chips, mini Yorkshire puddings with onion compote and mustard mash. And finish, rhubarb and rose petal jellies and smooth Irish coffee.

Your caterers are professionals and will have lots of interesting menu suggestions to suit your budget. But don't be afraid to make some suggestions of your own. You know your guests and their tastes best, and between you both you should be able to come up with a delicious menu to suit everyone.

WEDDING DRINKS

Champagne is the drink most associated with a wedding celebration and most of your guests will enjoy at least one glass, if only to toast the bride and groom after the speeches.

Strictly speaking champagne is available just from one particular region in France and anything else is sparkling wine. There is a lot of snobbery surrounding this most special drink and many couples feel that their guests will be offended unless they are offered 'the real thing'. What you choose is really up to your budget and your tastebuds.

Unless you are something of a champagne connoisseur, it is worth seeking the advice of an expert, either at your venue or a wine merchant and sample some of their recommendations. Brut on the label denotes a dry taste, sec is sweet and demi-sec is the sweetest. Pink champagne is particularly suited to a wedding and comes in a variety of colours from the softest pastel to a deep rose. Serve well chilled in tall flutes that maximize the bubbles.

Sparkling wine varies enormously in quality and price with the best being able to fool even the most determined of experts in blind tastings. The best quality sparkling wines come from Australia, New Zealand and California.

Your guests will expect to be offered both white and red wine, regardless of what you are eating. Be guided by the venue as to what they can offer. If you have a particular favourite that is not available, check corkage charges – where you provide your own wines but the venue charge per bottle to open and serve them. It may be worth buying your own from another source and adding on a corkage charge.

Make sure you order enough wine to serve all your guests. Many venues offer bottles on a sale or return basis, which means you don't have to pay for anything that has not been opened. As a guide, one bottle will serve about five glasses. You will also need plenty of soft drinks for non-drinkers, drivers and children.

Cocktail Hour

Turn your wedding reception into an A-list party with the inroduction of a few cocktails. Presentation is all-important so speak to your venue about glasses. Give each cocktail a suitably romantic name and decorate with fruit and flowers.

- **ABSOLUTELY FABULOUS**
  Shake 1 shot of vodka together with 2 shots of cranberry juice and ice. Strain into a martini glass and top up with champagne.

- **THE WEDDING CAKE**
  Blend together 2 shots light rum, 1 shot amaretto, 1 shot double cream, 1 shot milk, 3 shots pineapple juice, 1 shot cream of coconut. Garnish with chocolate chunks and ice.

- **ISLAND BREEZE**
  Shake together 2 shots of Malibu, 3 shots cranberry juice, 2 shots grapefruit juice with ice and strain into a tall glass.

- **FROZEN MARGARITA**
  Mix 2 shots Tequila, 1 shot Cointreau, 1 shot of freshly squeezed lime juice. Blend together with lots of ice until slushy.

- **LOVE JUNK**
  Shake together 1 shot vodka, 1 shot Midori melon liquer, 1 shot peach schnapps, 3 shots pressed apple juice. Strain into a tall ice-filled glass.

If your budget will stretch to such extravagances, a champagne fountain where filled, bowl-shaped champagne glasses are piled into a tower or a vodka luuge, which involves guests drinking neat vodka from an ice sculpture, are a memorable way to serve drinks.

The Dos of wedding drinks

- Do buy in advance if you can. Most weddings are announced months ahead of the date, so for a summer wedding buy in the January sales.
- Do buy the best sparkling wine you can rather than the cheapest champagne.
- Do serve your fizz from big bottles. Pulling out a Methuselah will impress your guests and saves opening eight smaller bottles!
- Do think about serving cocktails or an alcoholic punch, named after the bride and groom, to stretch the drinks budget. A cocktail is ideal to serve as guests arrive.
- Do serve wines your guests won't recognize. If you put well-known brands on the tables, they'll be able to work out exactly how much you have spent of them.
- Do go for the New World rather than Old World wines. They are more reliable and their fruitier flavours will go down better with your older guests.

… and the Don'ts

- Don't feel ashamed about hiring a van and buying discounted wines from warehouses or even from France.
- Don't serve different (ie: better) wines on the top table. People will notice and probably be offended.
- Don't automatically have waiters topping up glasses, give refills only when they are requested.
- Don't be embarrassed to organize a pay bar once the formal part of the reception is over.
- Don't provide spirits unless you are prepared for some of your guests to become very drunk.
- Don't forget to keep your drinks stores under lock and key. The more guests drink, the more they'll want to drink.

THE SEASIDE *wedding*

THE BEACH · BLUES · GREENS · SEASHELLS · SAND · SEAFOOD · INFORMALITY

JOANNE AGAR AND MARK ANDERSON, at Polhawn Fort in Cornwall. 'The main reason behind our choice of venue, apart from the fact it is a spectacular setting, is that we wanted the bride's family dog, Barney, to be able to come along to the wedding! Our aim was to create a beautiful, relaxed day where our friends could celebrate without feeling constrained by formalities. The Fort is right by the beach so the obvious theme for the day was the seaside. We used shells as placecard holders and our table centrepieces were made from shells and white flowers arranged in large glass containers of water – a simple and inexpensive idea which was very effective.

The wedding breakfast menu had a seafood theme with seafood crepes followed by a seafood medley with a raspberry and Drambuie roulade for dessert. The wedding cake was a mouthwatering three tiers of rich chocolate cake.

A surprise midnight firework display was probably the most magical moment for our guests. We were thankful for the weather, it had poured with rain for the week beforehand but for the wedding, the sun shone all day.'

Steal their wedding style

- Use blue and white tablecloths with centrepiece vases filled with sand and seashells
- Decorate window-sills and stairways with children's buckets filled with white, blue and lilac flowers
- Name each of the tables after a famous beach
- Serve mini paper cones filled with chips as hors d'oeuvres as guests arrive
- Set up an old-fashioned ice-cream stall serving traditional flavours of homemade ice-cream instead of having a formal dessert plate
- Create a sky blue cocktail and give it a beachy name. Serve complete with seaside umbrella

'We've both lived by the sea all our lives and it was an important part of our celebrations'

CHAPTER 8

THE WEDDING
cake

T HE FOCAL POINT of any wedding reception is the cake. Whether you chose a majestic tower of spun sugar or a pile of funky, individual fairy cakes, your cake has to be a feast for the eye as well as a treat for the tastebuds.

Think about your cake at the same time as you plan your reception menu, around three months before the wedding. Your caterer may have an in-house baker, or your venue can put you in touch with someone they have worked with before. Alternatively, you can find a specialist baker of your own to create something to suit your individual taste.

Many high street shops also produce well priced and good quality plain wedding cakes, in a variety of sizes so they can be stacked and then decorated professionally or accessorized with fresh flowers by your florist.

Above The perfect cake for a spring wedding decorated with sugar pearls and feathers. Left A plain shop bought cake can be bought and then iced professionally to match your colour scheme and save your budget. Right For a smaller wedding you can give guests individual cakes to either eat or take away with them. These mini-delights are also lovely to send to important guests who were unable to attend the wedding.

'Love is a friendship
set on fire'

CHOOSING A BAKER

Draw up short-list of potential cakemakers and visit each one armed with a list of questions. Do they charge a per-slice rate or for the whole cake? What's the delivery charge? Can they provide a cake stand and cake slice or will you have to provide these?

This is also the time to taste potential cakes because no matter how great a cake looks, it has to be delicious. Ask for a sample slice, the filling and the icing combinations that are available so that your tastebuds can help you choose.

An average three-tier cake will serve up to 100 guests and the more elaborate you want the design, the more expensive the cake. If you are having a large number of guests, your baker will probably advise you against more than four or five tiers since a very large cake is heavy and difficult to move. Extra slices can be kept in the kitchen and served once the main cake has been cut. Your baker may even suggest using dummy tiers made from cardboard and then iced to match the real tiers. Your guests will never know and it can save you money. Again extra slices can be kept in the kitchen for serving.

What's your style?

The traditional wedding cake is a rich fruit cake, much like christmas cake, with a buttercream filling and royal icing decorations. Your baker may also work with a fondant icing to wrap each tier providing a smooth surface for moulded flowers and piped details. How much decoration you have is limited only by the skill and imagination of your cakemaker. Fruits, flowers, doves, a miniature bride and groom who look just like you can all be made from sugar and marzipan and then painted to give very realistic results. Spun sugar made from pulled strands of caramelized sugar is another way to add a spectacular finishing touch to a cake, whipped into birds nests, domes and bows with a fairy-like quality.

Find your perfect cake

To help ensure your cake suits the occasion, looks amazing and tastes even better, put a tick against the descriptions that best suit your dream concoction.

STYLE
- ❏ Dramatic
- ❏ Ornate
- ❏ Regal
- ❏ Round
- ❏ Tiered, separated with columns
- ❏ Simple
- ❏ Traditional
- ❏ Unique

SHAPE
- ❏ Fairycakes
- ❏ Heart
- ❏ Rectangular
- ❏ Round
- ❏ Square
- ❏ Tiered, stacked

COLOURS
- ❏ White
- ❏ Yellow
- ❏ Peach
- ❏ Pink
- ❏ Gold or silver
- ❏ Other

DECORATION
- ❏ Cake topper
- ❏ Fresh Flowers
- ❏ Chocolate curls
- ❏ Gold leaf
- ❏ Sugar flowers

FILLINGS
- ❏ Chocolate
- ❏ Liqueurs
- ❏ Truffle
- ❏ White chocolate
- ❏ Mousse

NUMBER OF SERVINGS
- ❏ 0–50
- ❏ 50–100
- ❏ 100–150
- ❏ 150–200
- ❏ 200+

TALKING CAKES

It will help you to appreciate what your cakemaker is suggesting if you understand some of the jargon used in baking. Here is some of the common cake terminology.

BASKETWEAVE: a piping technique that features interwoven lines, like a basket

BUTTERCREAM: a smooth, creamy icing that stays soft so is easy to cut. Can be used as a filling or for decorations.

DRAGEES: edible sugar balls coated with silver or gold and used for decorations

FONDANT: a sweet, elastic icing that's rolled with a rolling pin and draped over a cake forming a smooth, firm base for decorations

GANACHE: a sweet, rich chocolate and cream mixture that is denser than mousse but not quite a fudge. Used for icing or fillings

GUM PASTE: a sugar and cornstarch mixture that is used to make realistic-looking flowers and decorations. These can last for years and are edible (but not that tasty)

MARZIPAN: a paste made from ground almonds, sugar and egg whites that can be made into all sort of decorations. It can also be rolled flat and used in sheets like fondant

PILLARS: tier separators available in various lengths depending on how high your want your cake stacked

PIPING: decorations and patterns applied using a pastry bag and variously shaped tips

ROYAL ICING: a type of icing made with egg white and sugar that is piped to create beading, bows, flowers and latticework. It dries hard

WHIPPED CREAM: a heavy cream that is sometimes used as a filling. It is not recommended as icing and doesn't suit hot weather

*Above An amazing dessert-style wedding cake made from dark chocolate sponge, white chocolate curls and fresh fruit. **Right** Four relatively simple stacked wedding cakes that have been transformed with sugar and fresh flowers. If you want to incorporate fresh flowers into the cake decoration, ask your florist to chat to your cakemaker beforehand to find out how the cake is being made, the shape and overall size so she can think about the perfect flowers to match.*

TYPES OF WEDDING CAKE

Traditional tiers

The most formal of the wedding cake styles where small Grecian-style pillars are set four square between each tier.

American stack

This is where the tiers of the cake sit directly on top of one another with no pillars in between each one. This is a more contemporary look and used at modern weddings.

Fairy cakes

Individual fairy cakes, one for each guest, are piled into a tower. This makes a fantastic centrepiece and suits a fun, informal wedding. But don't forget you won't be able to have the traditional cake cutting ceremony.

Croquembouche

Originally from France this involves a tower of choux pastry profiteroles covered in a rich toffee sauce and spun sugar. The bride and groom can cut it (carefully) in the usual way.

If you are buying an undecorated cake from a high street, the easiest way of transforming it into something special is to ask your florist to decorate it with fresh flowers that match your colour scheme. Wrap the base of each tier with a strip of inch width ribbon to hide the joins between each layer.

As an alternative to the traditional fruit cake, which is not to everyone's taste, it is quite usual to order a cake made from chocolate or sponge with a variety of fillings, including some exotic and even alcoholic concoctions. Less traditional cakes often take the place of dessert and can be made with fruit and cream if you prefer. Just remember that this type of cake won't travel so cannot be boxed and sent to absent friends and relatives.

Wedding cake toppers

- A miniature bride and groom
- A pair of white doves
- Ask your florist about making a tiny, colour-themed posy of fresh flowers
- Sugar roses
- A sugar crown
- An oversize bow in colour-themed organza

PRESENT AND CORRECT

Unless otherwise asked, your cakemaker will bring the cake to the reception on a plain, usually silver coloured, cardboard base. For a more personal touch, ask your baker to cover a wooden board in fondant and decorate this to match the cake, or ask them to write your names in icing around the base. For a more traditional display, your venue may be able to supply a silver cakestand – just make sure it is big enough to fit the base of the cake.

The cake should be placed on a table where all your guests can see it, either in the centre of the room or at one end. Just make sure it is positioned so it cannot be easily knocked and there is enough room to move around it with ease.

You want the cake to be the centre of attention so don't go overboard decorating the table it sits on. A good quality white linen tablecloth, a fan of silver cake forks, linen napkins or a beautiful cake slice tied with a bow should suffice. A light scattering of fresh rose petals always looks pretty, particularly if your cake has a floral theme.

Above An amazing four tier fruit cake decorated with white chocolate curls and trailed with fresh roses and ivy. **Right** An interesting stacked design using a square base and circular tiers is covered with a mixture of fresh flower heads. **Left** A traditional cake supported on columns with an intricate sugar 'string of pearls' design and chocolate curls shaped into flowers.

CUTTING THE CAKE

After the dessert and usually before the coffee is served is the traditional time to cut the cake. The best man announces this is about to take place or cues the band to play a brief fanfare to gather guests around the cake table. Apart from being a wonderful opportunity for photographs, it is good luck for the bride and groom to cut the first slice of cake. The bride holds the knife with the groom's hand over hers. It is also tradition for the bride to feed her groom a bite of cake before the caterers take over and cut and serve the rest of the cake to the guests with coffee.

If the wedding cake is doubling up as dessert, it is quite usual for it to be served with fresh fruit, ice cream or cream.

If you want to follow tradition, it is possible to wrap and freeze a tier of the cake to enjoy at a later date. Tradition dictates this should be at your first child's christening or on your first anniversary. Double check with your cakemaker that the ingredients they have used are suitable for this treatment, it may be that you have to celebrate your first month's anniversary instead!

If you are having a themed wedding, theme the wedding cake to suit the occasion. As themed weddings tend to be less formal, have fun with your cake and ask your baker to stretch their imagination. These three wonderful creations were made for a black and white wedding, an Indian-inspired afternoon tea party and the butterfly adorned cake was for a high summer garden party wedding.

THE COUNTRY HOUSE *wedding*

CONTEMPORARY · INDIVIDUAL · VENUE WOW FACTOR · WHITE & GOLD · WINNIE THE POOH

ANTONIA SOUTHGATE AND JEREMY SALSBY at Castle Ashby, Northamptonshire. 'We wanted to create a wedding that reflected our individual characteristics while embracing our spiritual beliefs. Castle Ashby had the necessary 'wow factor' we were looking for, and from a practical point of view, the ceremony and reception could be held in the same place. Close friends and family even stayed the night in some of the bedrooms which made the wedding last all weekend.

It took weeks in libraries finding the readings we wanted and we spent many evenings listening to CDs until we found the perfect music to accompany the ceremony. I walked up the aisle crushing lavender pods underfoot to the song *It Had to Be You* sung by one of our best friends. One of our readings was *Us Two* from Winnie the Pooh, which brought a tear to the eye of most of the female guests! We wrote our own wedding vows incorporating the love, trust and respect that we feel for one another into every line.

Our guests dined on fillet of sole followed by baked rack of lamb with garlic mash and finished off with individual bread and butter puddings and cinnamon ice-cream. Our wedding cake was the most amazing white and dark Belgian chocolate affair, which weighed an incredible eight stones.

The best value for money for me was my hair and make-up artist. I would gladly have paid double for the calming effect she had on me whilst everything else was going wedding crazy.'

Steal their wedding style

- Buy a few potted white orchids, you only need a few to make a lot of impact
- Choose meaningful vows – a civil ceremony gives you lots of opportunities to personalize the words
- Do your research, well chosen music says a lot about your personalities
- Add a spectacular feature, like an amazing cake, for photo opportunities and to give guests a talking point
- Entertain guests with a wedding quiz to see who knows most about the happy couple. The winning table gets a bottle of bubbly
- Think about a restricted guest list, this can mean the difference between a so-so and a wow venue

'Our wedding was very relaxed, we didn't stop smiling all day'

THE WHITE
pages

Over the past ten years whilst editor of *You & Your Wedding* I have come across a huge range of companies associated with the wedding industry. Listed here are many of my favourite suppliers – the people the magazine have found to be creative, reliable and able to provide the quality of work that I can happily now recommend to you. A large proportion of the companies are based in the London area but don't let this put you off. Many will travel to other parts of the country and many offer a mail order service. Don't be afraid to ring and discuss your requirements. Make a list of questions you need to ask then request a brochure so you can browse this at home. These people make a living from weddings just like yours and they want you, their customers, to be happy with the services they provide. The more information you can give about what you like and how much you want to spend will all help to ensure that you get the best from everyone you contact. Happy shopping!

UK Contacts

ARTIFICIAL FLOWERS
Sia
0870-608 6060
The Dulwich Trader
020-8761 3457
Texstyle World
0141-304 7217

BALLOON DECORATIONS
NABAS, The Balloon Association
01989-762204
www.nabas.co.uk
Balloons for Occasions
0870-777 8797
www.balloonsforoccasions.com

BRIDAL FABRICS
Bridal Fabrics & Laces
0115-946 0766
Bridal Laces and Fabrics
0115-958 6695
Thai and Indian Silks
01635-298294
Simons, The Fabric People
01254-382029
www.theweddingpeople.co.uk
VV Rouleaux (ribbons, trimmings)
020-7224 5179
Wedding Fabrics
01530-415007

CANDLES
candlesontheweb
www.candlesontheweb.co.uk

Price's Candles
01234-264500
Wedding Candles
353 1 8455200
www.weddingonline.ie/weddingcandle

CAKEMAKERS
Amato Wedding Cakes
020-7734 5733
Bettys of Harrogate
01904-659142
British Sugarcraft Guild
020-8859 6953
www.bsguk.org
Celebration Cakes
0118-9424 581
www.celebcakes.com
Choccywoccydoodah
01273-329462
www.choccywoccydoodah.com
Elizabeth Lyle
01892-740354
www.elizabethlylecakes.com
Funky Cakes from Heaven
01435 874894
The Icing on the Cake
01895 622064
www.icingoncake.co.uk
Imaginative Icing
01904-654635
www.imaginativeicing.co.uk
Konditor & Cook
020-7261 0456
The Little Venice Cake Company
020-7486 5252

The Little Wedding Cake Company
01932-872115
www.littlecakes.co.uk
Linda Fripp
01722-718518
Maison Blanc
020-7224 0228
A Matter of Taste
020-8550 3306
www.amatterof.com
Rachel Mount Cakes
020-8672 9333
Pat-a-Cake-Pat-a-Cake
020-7485 0006
Patisserie Valerie
020-7437 3466
Purita Hyam
01403-891518
Slattery Patissier & Chocolatier
0161-767 9303
www.slattery.co.uk
Savoir Design
020-8788 0808

CATERING COMPANIES
Admirable Crichton
020-7326 3800
www.admirable-crichton.co.uk
Blistering Barbeques
020-7720 7678
www.blisteringgroup.co.uk
Bovingdons
020-8874 8032
www.bovingdons.co.uk

Chocolate Fondue
01883-625905
Create Food
020-8870 1717
www.createfood.co.uk
Delectable Feasts
020-7585 0512
www.delectablefeasts.co.uk
Jalapeno
020-7639 6500
www.jalapenolondon.co.uk
Mosimann's Party Service
020-7326 8344
www.mosimann.co.uk
Mustard Catering
020-7840 5900
www.mustardcatering.co.uk
Norman & Hatwell Caterers
01963-362856
Turtle Soup
020-7653 6688
www.turtlesoup.co.uk
Urban Kitchen
020-7286 1700
Williams Kitchen
01453-832240
CEREMONIES
Baptists Union
01235-517700
British Humanist Association
020-7430 0908
www.humanism.org.uk
Church of England
020-7898 1000
www.church-of-england.org

Church of Scotland
0131-225 5722
General Register Office
of England and Wales
0151-471 4200
www.ons.gov.uk
General Register Office for Jersey
01534-502335
General Register Office
for Northern Ireland
028-9025 2000
General Register Office for
Scotland
0131-314 4447
Greek Archdiocese
020-7723 4787
Jewish Marriage Council
020-8203 6311
Marriage Care (Catholic)
020-7371 1341
www.marriagecare.org.uk
Methodist Church
020-7222 8010
United Reform Church
020-7916 2020

CHAIR COVERS & LINENS
Cover Story
01206-791128
Event Angels Chair Covers
0115-849 6904
www.event-angels.co.uk
Host with Style
020-8893 4823
www.hostwithstyle.co.uk

Mediterrananean Occasions
020-8883 2493
www.mediterraneanoccasions.co.uk
Northfields
020-8880 5555
Snape-Drape Hire
01568-616638   www.snapdrape.co.uk

CONFETTI
Bougainvillea
01404-811467
www.passionforpetals.com
Natural Hop Confetti
01531-670849
Rhapsody in Bloom
01792-893214
The Real Flower Confetti Co
01386-555045
www.confettidirect.co.uk
The Very Nice Company
01884-251551
www.theverynicecompany.com
Trousseau
01332-875048

DISPOSABLE CAMERAS
Argos
www.argos.co.uk
Confetti
0870-840 6060
www.confetti.co.uk
Twenty One C
0845-1303606
www.disposablecamerashop.co.uk
/weddings

Forever Memories

01384-878111

Wedding Cameras

020-8755 7950

www.weddingcameras.co.uk

Doves

The White Dove Company

020-8508 1414

www.thewhitedovecompany.co.uk

FAVOURS

Amanda Lincoln

01438-861015

Corr Ranges

01202-740909

Belle Bomboniere

0121-421 3182

www.bellebomboniere.co.

La Bomboniera

020-7437 2916

Carte Blanche

01943-600283

Diddy Gilly

0161-643 8132

www.diddygilly.co.uk

Love Hearts

0800-9700480

www.lovehearts.com

Stem Jewellery

01560-483461

www.stemjewellery.com

The Very Nice Company

01884-251551

www.theverynicecompany.com

The White House

01905-381149

To Have and To Hold

01326-574656

Totally Crackers

0113-278 5525

www.totally-crackers.com

Truly Madly Deeply

0116-259 0092

UK Wedding Favours

www.ukweddingfavours.com

Wedding Fortune Cookies

020-8932 7932

FLORISTS AND FLORAL DECORATION

Angel Flowers

020-7704 6312

British Retail and

Prof Florists Association

01942-719127

John Carter

020-7731 5146

Mathew Dickinson

020-7503 0456

The Event People

01886-830088

Flower and Plant Association

020-7738 8044

Sam Joseph at Flower

020-8364 9901

Robbie Honey

020-7720 3777

In Water

020-7724 9985

Sophie Hanna

020-7720 1756

Mary Jane Vaughan
020-7385 8400

Jane Packer
020-7486 1300

Paula Pryke
020-7837 7373

Pollen Count
020-7602 5500

Pressed Flower Design
01273-424299

Tiger Rose
01730-829989

Veevers Carter
020-7735 8040

Wild at Heart
020-7704 6312

FIREWORKS

Aurora Fireworks
0800-9756573
www.aurorafireworks.co.uk

Atmospheric Pyrotechnics
01225-764189

1st Galaxy Fireworks
0870-4430210
www.galaxy-fireworks.co.uk

Firework Store
020-7223 5496
www.fireworkstore.co.uk

G-Force Fireworks
01905-422554

Highlight Polytechnics
01928-566677
www.fireworks.eu.com

JackFlash Fireworks
01939-200444

www.jackflashdireworks.co.uk

Laser Visuals
01622-662025
www.laservisuals.co.uk

Merlin Fireworks
0800-3891694
www.merlin-fireworks.co.uk

Northern Lights
01225-764189
www.nlfireworks.com

Rocket Pyrotechnics
01474-707590
www.rocketpyro.com

The Firework Co.
01884-840504
www.thefireworkco.co.uk

Wedding Day Fireworks
0800 018 9560
www.celebrationdisplays.co.uk

HENS & STAGS

Bash!
0800-3285628

Dynamic Days
0845-6441167
www.dynamic.co.uk

www.PartyParties.co.uk
01442-834993

www.stagparty.co.uk
0870-7517377

www.henparty.co.uk
0870-7517377

Weekends by Design
0870-321 9600
www.weekendsbydesign.co.uk

WEDDING DRESS STORAGE

The Empty Box Company
01306-740193
www.emptybox.co.uk

HIRE COMPANIES

Jones Catering Equipment Hire
020-820 0600

HSS Event Hire
0845-722 2000

Northfields
020-8880 5555

Top Table Hire
01327-260575

ICE SCULPTURES

Up Periscopes Ice Sculpture
01580-240701
www.up-periscope.org.uk

The Ice Box
020-7498 0800

Ice Creations
01580-892977
www.icecreations.tv

MARQUEES & LIGHTING

Bedouin Tent Company
07941-370241 www.beduointents.com

Brookfield Marquees
01798-342255

Complete Events
020-7610 1770
www.marqueecelebrations.co.uk

Crescent Moon
0800-083 8480

Lightech
01260-223666
www.lightech.co.uk
The Maypole
01227-751233
www.maypolemarquee.co.uk
The Main Event
01580-860318
www.themainevent.co.uk
The Marquee Company
01788-822922
Orchard Marquee Hire
0800-0371889
www.orchardmarquees.co.uk
Raj Tent Company
020-7376 9066
www.rajtentclub.com
The Made Up Textiles Association
01827-52337
www.muta.org.uk

MOBILE BARS
020-8446 6900
Cocktailmaker
020-8886 2720
London Bar Services
020-8950 4455
www.londonbarservices.com
Occasional Butler
020-8880 6888
The Booze Brothers
020-8207 4150

MUSIC & ENTERTAINMENT
Abba Explosion
01253-640529

Ace of Hearts Wedding Casino
020-8767 2267
Alive Network Entertainment
01782-740777
Dixon Agency
0870-438 8888
Duende Music
020-88877 3831
www.duendemusic.co.uk
England Music Agency
07071-202989
Function Junction
020-8900 5959
www.functionjunction.co.uk
Robin Williamson
01280-812266
www.caricaturist.net
Mechanical Fracture
(human statues) 020-8785 0363
Music Finders
01273-603633
Sam Entertainment
01732-832244
www.samentertainments.co.uk
Sternberg Clarke
020-8877 1102
www.sternbergclarke.co.uk
The Magic Circle
www.themagiccircle.co.uk
The Wedding Music Company
020-8293 3392
www.weddingmusic.co.uk
Wellpleased (inflatable disco dome)
0113-244 2720

PHOTOGRAPHY & VIDEO
British Institute of Professional Photography
01920-464011
www.bipp.com
Guild of Wedding Photographers
0161-926 9367
Master Photographers Association
01325-356555
www.mpauk.com
Society of Wedding & Portrait Photographers
01745-815030
www.swpp.com
Association of Professional Videomakers
01529-421717
MOBILE CRECHES
Crechendo
020-8675 6611
The Mobile Creche Company
020-7736 0022
The Wedding Creche Service
01483-202490

TOASTMASTERS AND SPEECHES
National Association of Toastmasters
01322-554342
www.natuk.com
Speech Write
0118-971 4702
Speech-Writers
www.speech-writers.com

WEDDING CO-ORDINATION / PARTY PLANNERS

Alternative Occasions
Liz Sexton
01932-872115

Asian Wedding Services
020-8470 1177

A Perfect Day
01780-410487

Carole Sobell
020-8200 8111

Chelsea Wedding Consultant
020-7581 3738

Champagne Events
0976-386162

Deborah Dwek
020-8446 9501
www.deborahdwekweddings.co.uk

Dreamaker
01282-770425

Dr Party
0870-900 0414
www.drparty.com

Event, Event
020-7242 6455

Happily Hitched
07951-577782
www.happilyhitched.com

JD Events
020-7436 4361

Jonathan Seaward Organisation
020-8996 6699

Fifth Element Event Design
020-7610 8630

Weddings Co-ordinated, Rani Bain
020-7308 5626

Linda Magistris
020-8871 4865

The National Wedding Information Service
0800-783 7452

The Wedding Event Company
01536-744141

Scottish Wedding Services
0131-477 4743
www.getmarriedinscotland.co.uk

Special Events
01789-490503

Siobhan Craven Robins
020-7481 4338
www.siobhancraven-robins.co.uk

Something New
01427-754994
www.somethingnew.com

WEDDING HAIR AND MAKE-UP

The Body Shop
01903-731500

Bridal Hair & Make-up
01342-850 895

Chanel for Brides
020-7493 3836

Classic Bridal Make-Up Co
01883-347808

Clinique
020-7409 6951

Elle Au Naturel
01306-713660

Estee Lauder for Brides
0800-525501

Make-up & Hair Design
01206-299548

Max Factor for Brides
0800-169 1302

Molton Brown
020-7625 6550

WEDDING INSURANCE

Events Insurance Services
01425-470360
www.events-insurance.co.uk

Debenhams Insurance Plan
01603-463084

Marks & Spencer
0800-316 5985

Wedding Plan
0870-7744055
www.weddingplaninsurance.com

Weddingsurance
0118-957 5491
www.weddingsurance.co.uk

WEDDING STATIONERY

Belly Button Designs
0161-448 9333
www.bellybuttondesigns.com

CCA
01772-663030

Jo Blue
0800-301234
www.joblue.com
Debenhams
020-7408 4444

Giggle
01873-850141

Hitched
www.hitched-stationery.co.uk

Libra Designs
01234-376165
Little Cherub Design
01609-773239
Marks & Spencer Stationery
www.marksandspencer.com/giftregistry
Scrumptious Design
020-8985 5944
Smythson of Bond Street
020-7629 8668
Silver Nutmeg
01992-501464
www.silvernutmeg.com
Taylormade Card Company
023-8055 9400
Elspeth J Walker
020-8342 9110
WHSmith Wedding Stationery
01772-662810

VENUE FINDERS
The Function Room
08702-030403
www.thefunctionroom.net
Nobles Venue Guide
01580-752404
www.noblesvenues.com
www.perfectvenue.com
www.weddings.co.uk/wvenues
www.net-weddings.co.uk
www.highlandcastleweddings.com

WEDDINGS ABROAD
AND HONEYMOONS
Airtours
01706-212888

British Airways Holidays
0870-608 2244
First Choice
0161-742 2262
French Riviera Weddings
00 33 620 798 890
Get Married in Tuscany
020-7460 846
www.get-married.co.uk
Italian Connection
020-7486 6890
Italia Romantica
020-8830 2090
Kuoni
01306-747007
Sunset Faraway Holidays
020-8498 9922
Thomson
0161-911 8338
Tradewinds
0870-751 0009
Unijet Weddings Department
0870-24 24 247

WEDDING TRANSPORT
American '50's Cars
01268-735914
Bespokes Classic Cars
01923-250250
Cabair Helicopters
020-8953 4411
Cinderella's Magic Coach
01491-413322
Cute Classics & Executive 1
01904-758758

Horizon Hotair Balloons
01420-520505
La-De-Da
01782-329038
London Central Buses
020-8646 1747
Nostalgiabus
020-8640 6668
Traditional Horse Drawn Carriages
01754-880590
White Wedding Taxi Service
01959-575224

WEDDING SHOWS
The National Wedding Shows
0870-730 0064
www.nationalweddingshow.co.uk
The UK Wedding Shows
01704-882 050

WEDDING WEBSITES
www.blissfulweddings.co.uk
www.confetti.co.uk
www.hitched.co.uk
www.honeymoonsupreme.co.uk
www.irishweddingsonnline.com
www.kodakweddings.co.uk
www.scottishweddings.org
www.weddingguideUK.com
www.weddingpages.co.uk
www.webwedding.co.uk
www.weddings-abroad.com
www.welshweddingsonline.com

WEDDING DRESSES
MADE TO MEASURE DESIGNS
Allison Blake
020-7732 9322
Amanda Wakeley Sposa
020-7590 9108
Anna Christina
020-8527 7001
Sharon Bowen
01260-271269
Caroline Castigliano
020-7636 8212
Catherine Davighi
01604-60122
Chanticleer
01242-226502
David Fielden
020-7351 0067
Alan Hannah
020-8882 0007
Trudy Hanson
020-7792 1300
Hayley J
01743-235140
Hollywood Dreams
020-8801 9797
London Designer Bridal Room
020-7434 3966
Linea Raffaelli
00 32 13771476
Modern Bride
01372-469749
Morgan Davies
020-73543414
Suzanne Neville
020-8423 3161

Jenny Packham
020-7267 3221
Caroline Parkes
020-8646 4916
Stewart Parvin
020-7235 1125
Ian Stuart
01908-615599
Donna Salado
01604-792869
Tracy Connop
01242-539353
Wedding Dress at Harrods
020-7730 1234
Ritva Westenius
020-7706 2900
Robinson Valentine
020-7409 2900
Vera Wang at The Wedding Shop
020-7838 0171
Wizard of Gos
020-7938 1025

OFF THE PEG WEDDING AND
BRIDESMAIDS' DRESSES
Berkertex Bride
020-7287 7909
BHS
020-7262 3288
Castigliano Collections
020-7766 0100
Paloma Blanca
01274-598380
Debenhams
020-7408 4444

Sarah Danielle
01908 615246
Monsoon
020-7313 3000
Mori Lee
01476-591306
Ronald Joyce
020-7269 3221
Pronuptia
020-7419 9014
Sincerity
01908 615511
Veromia
020-8554 6436
Watters & Watters
020-7766 0100
Young Bride & Groom
01923-249664

BRIDAL BAGS
Angelina Colarusso
020-8398 0065
Camilla Ridley
020-7221 7329
Clare Musgrove
01902-827126
Dollargrand
020-7794 3028
Emily Jo Gibbs
020-7490 8834
Emma Hope
020-7259 9566
Louisa Scott
020-7565 4100
Lulu Guinness
020-7221 9686

BRIDAL GLOVES
Cornelia James
020-7499 9423
Dents
01985-212291

BRIDAL JEWELLERY
Alter Ego
01727-862762
Angela Hale
020-7495 1920
Angie Gooderham
020-7488 0935
Cavendish French Recollections
0800-731 4389
Cherry Chau at Harvey Nichols
020-7235 1857
Coleman Douglas Pearls
020-7373 3369
Designs on You
0113-269 6734
Dominic Walmsley
020-7250 0125
Dower & Hall
020-7589 8474
Elizabeth Edema
020-7229 2564
Jeremy Hoye
01273-777207
Jewel In The Crown
020-7494 0319
Lovely Fairy
020-7431 0279
Malcolm Morris
020-7916 8060

Mikey
020-7287 1232
Noel
020-7730 2817
Sophie Jonas
01707-656531
Swanky
01273-818390
Tallulah
023-8025 5185
Tarina Tarantino at Harrods
020-7730 1234
BRIDAL SHOES
Anello & Davide
020-7225 2468
Christian Louboutin
020-7823 2234
Diane Hassall
020-8223 0505
Emma Hope
020-7259 9566
Fenaroli for Regalia at Morgan-Davies
020-7354 3414
Gabriella & Lucido
01392-207030
Gamba
020-8903 8177
Hanna Goldman
020-7739 2690
Helen Creedy Smith at Edwina Ibbotson
020-7498 5390
HKE
01323-728988

Jean-Claude Bidi
020-7419 2330

Jimmy Choo
020-7235 0242

Jones Bootmaker
0800-163519

Joseph Azagury
020-7259 6887

LK Bennett
020-7491 3005

Kate Pennington
020-8203 2647

Meadows
01603-219174

Office
020-8838 4447

Rainbow Club
01392-207030

TIARAS AND HEADDRESSES
Alter Ego
01727-862762

Andrew Prince
020-7265 9113

Angelina Colarusso
020-8398 0065

Bijoux Heart
01709-363318

Blossom
01252-851733

Butler & Wilson
020-7409 2955

Halo & Co
01283-704305

Irresistible
01403-871449

Jewel In The Crown
020-7494 0319

Leigh-Anne McCague
01622-890922

Mariana Christodoulou
020-8364 3754

Palmer Design
01604-686384

Petals International
0113-266 0388

Philippa Eyland
020-7729 7350

Polly Edwards
01903-882127

Rachel Trevor-Morgan
020-7839 8927

Slim Barrett
020-7354 9393

Veils Carousel
0115-911 0446

Cocoa
01242-233588

Irresistible
01403-871449

Joyce Jackson Bridal Veils
01745-343689

Linzi Jay
01254-665104

MENSWEAR , TO BUY AND HIRE
Anthony Formalwear
01277-651140

Burton Menswear Nationwide
0800-731 8283

Debenhams Nationwide
020-7408 4444

Formal Affair Wales/Midlands
0800-9178092

Gary Anderson London
020-7224 2241

Geoffrey (Tailor) Scotland
0141-331 2388

Greenwoods Nationwide
01943-876100

Heaphys Midlands
0808-100 2498

Lords Formal Wear
020-7363 1033

Losners Home Counties
020-8800 9281

Masterhand Nationwide
01480-460400

Moss Bros Nationwide
020-7447 7200

Pronuptia Nationwide
01444-417185

Youngs Hire at Suits You
Nationwide
020-8327 3005

WEATHER FORECAST
Northern Ireland
09001-600316

Scotland
09001-600318

North-East England
09001-600285

North-West England
09001-600286

Wales
09001-600343

The Midlands
09001-600344
East Anglia
09001-600347
London & South-East
09001-600348
South-West England
09001-600349

TOURIST INFORMATION
English Tourism Council
020-8563 3000
Scottish Tourist Board
0131-332 2433
Welsh Tourist Board
029-2049 9909
Northern Ireland Tourist Board
028-9024 6609

SPAS WITH PAMPERING PACKAGES
Bliss
020-7584 3888
The Christian Dior Spa
020-7201 1699
The Dorchester Spa
020-7629 8888
Elizabeth Arden Red Door
020-7629 4488
The Sanctuary
020-7420 5151
Bath Spa Hotel, Bath
01225-444424
Cedar Falls, Somerset
01823-433233
Champneys, Hertfordshire
01442-291111

Chewton Glen, Hampshire
01425-275341
Hanbury Manor, Hertfordshire
01920-487722
Henlow Grange, Bedfordshire
01462-811111
Hoar Cross Hall, Staffordshire
01283-575671
Ragdale Hall, Leicestershire
01664-434831
Springs Hydro, Leicestershire
01530-273873

US Contacts

BEAUTY
Patricia Bowden-Luccardi
203.324.1463
Kim DePaolera
973.942.4927
Rick Teal
212.206.0901

CAKE TOPPERS
Arturo Diaz
214.760.8707
Cory Lewis
305.296.9323
Gia Grosso
212.627.7827
Laura Wilensky
845.338.2199
Perfect Couple
212.255.4841

CALLIGRAPHY

Anna Pinto
201.656.7402

The Calligraphy Company
201.866.1985

Calligraphy Studios
212.964.6007

Harriet Rose Calligraphy & Design
212.663.4564

Jay Greenspan
212.496.5399

Jonathan Kremer
610.664.9625

K2 Design
214.522.2344

Kevin Karl
817.926.2888

Papineau
510.339.2301

Pendragon Ink
508.234.6843

Richard Jordan
212.255.4511

Special Letters
310.316.1533

Washington Calligrapher's Guild
301.897.8637

CANDLES

Barker Co.
800.543.0601

Candelier
415.989.8600

The Candle Shop
212.989.0148

The Candlestick
800.972.6777

General Wax & Candle Company
818.765.6357
www.genwax.com

Hurd Beeswax Candles
707.963.7211
800.977.7211

Ilume
213.782.0342

Lamplight Farms
414.781.9590

Nelson Candles
800.323.5901

Perin-Mowen
212.219.3937
214.748.2128

Sample House & Candle Shop
214.599.0335
817.429.7857

Wicks & Sticks
281.874.0800

CONFECTIONERS

Candy Conversation Hearts
800.725.6763
www.bridallink.com

Chocolates by Bernard Callebaut
800.526.6553
www.bernardchocolate.com

Doughnut Planet
212.505.3700

Economy Candy
800.352.4544
212.254.1832

Eleni's Cookies
212.255.7990

English Cottage Candies
717.866.4789

The Gift Factory
818.365.6619
800.284.2422

Hammond Candies
88.226.3999

Haute Chocolature
212.751.9591

JLH European Trading
415.626.3672

Johnson Candy
617.776.6255
www.johnsoncandy.com

La Maison du Chocolat
800.988.5632
www.lamaisonduchocolat.com

Tea and Cake Confections
212.645.2742
www.teaandcake.com

Teuscher Chocolates of Switzerland
212.751.8482

Tom and Sally's Handmade Chocolates
800.827.0800
802.254.4200
www.tomandsallys.com

The Truffle Mistress
212.780.9771

Toraya
212.861.1700

CONSULTANTS AND EVENT PLANNERS

Along Came Mary
213.931.9082

An Event to Remember
516.593.4164

Bruce Southworth
847.695.6070

Celebrations
901.525.5223

Connie Kerns
510.339.3370

Creative Parties
301.654.9292

Gale Sliger
214.637.5566

Grand Luxe
201.327.2333

Great Performances
212.727.2424

Jacque Designs
310.859.6424

Judith Schwartz
212.570.9818

Kate Edmonds
212.366.4447

Linda Alpert
847.831.9891

Lori Draper
406.961.5580

Marcy Blum Associates
212.688.3057

Margo Bouanchaud
225.952.9010

McCall Associates
415.552.8550

Nina Austin
214.871.3634

Parties, Parties
415.331.0544

Party Concepts
310.820.2255

Perfect Parties
212.563.2040

The Wedding Resource
415.928.8621

FLORAL DESIGNERS

Andrew Pascoe
516.922.9561

Arrangement
305.576.9922

Ateliér A Work Shop
214.750.7622

Baumgarten Krueger
414.276.2382

Bloom
212.620.5666

Blossoms
248.644.4411

Bomarzo
415.771.9111

Botanicals on the Park
800.848.7674

Brady's Floral Design
602.945.8776
800.782.6508

Charles Radcliff
713.522.9100

Cornucopia
212.594.8944
www.cornucopiaflowers.com

The Crest of Fine Flowers
888.401.9856

Curtis Godwin
910.484.4547

Cynthia's Creations
303.841.5381

Designs by Jodi
847.816.6661

Devorah Nussenbaum et Verdure
510.548.7764

Elizabeth House
704.342.3919

Elizabeth Ryan
212.995.1111

Enflora
317.634.3434

English Garden
615.352.0094

Fujikami Florist, Inc.
808.537.9948

Friendly Flower Gallery
919.596.8747

Garden Center
801.595.6622

Heffernan Morgan
773.782.0800

Hibiscus
816.891.0808

Larkspur
612.332.2140

Palmer-Kelly
317.923.9903

Perfect Presentations
504.522.7442

Peter A. Chopin Florist, Inc.
504.891.4455

Rosewood Florists
803.256.8351

INFORMATION SOURCES
American Institute for
Conservation
202.452.9545
American Rental Association
800.334.2177
Association for Bridal
Consultants
203.355.0164
Flower council of Holland
516.621.3625
Hagstrom Map & Travel Center
212.398.1222
www.hagstrommaps.com
The Knot
www.theknot.com
on-line source guide
National Center for Health
Statistics
301.458.4636
www.cdc.goc
national data & info, wedding licenses
National Limousine Association
800.NLA.7007
Neighborhood Cleaners
Association
212.967.3002
Society for Calligraphy
213.931.6146
Teleflora
310.231.9199
The Wedding Library
212.327.0100

www.weddinglibrary.net
research boutique

MUSIC AND DANCE
Archive of Contemporary Music
212.226.6967
www.archmusic.com
Baguette Quartet
510.528.3723
Bud Maltin
201.444.7001
212.447.6543
www.budmaltin.com
Curtis Music & Entertainment
908.352.3131
El Mariachi
215.567.6060
Festival Brass
214.328.9330
Hank Lane Music and
Productions
212.767.0600
516.829.4111
Janet King
516.671.4519
classical harpist
Jeff Robbins
214.414.2645
jazz trios to contemporary quartets
Ladies Choice String Quartet
310.391.3762
Music In The Air
212.946.1563
800.332.9705
www.musicintheair.com
jazz ensemble

New York City Swing
718.848.9442
Paul Lindemeyer Trio
845.693.9055
classic jazz
Peggy Cone Entertainment
212.734.1361
vocalist, 30s–40s songs a specialty
Peter Duchin
212.972.2260
orchestra

PHOTOGRAPHY AND VIDEOGRAPHY
Aimee Rentmeester
323.878.0044
Amber Productions
805.964.4533
Babboni's Creative Imaging
414.328.3211
Bachrach Studio
800.277.9077
212.755.6233
Bresner Studios
215.546.7277
Cheryl Klauss
212.431.3569
Cilento
414.964.6161
Fisher Photography
802.496.5215
541.387.5954
www.madriver.com/fisher
Frank Lopez Photography
877.321.5411

Gruber Photographers
212.262.9777
www.gruberphotographers.com
Hal Slifer
800.234.7755
617.787.7910
Hi-Tech PhotoImaging
516.931.8631
Jack Caputo
310.273.6181
James French Photography
214.368.0990
Jamie Bosworth Photography
503.246.5378
Jenny Bissell
440.247.7988
John Dolan
212.462.2598
John Tilley Photography
214.358.4747
www.johntilleyphotography.com

STATIONERY
Aesthete
401.846.6324
Alpine Creative Group
800.289.6507
212.989.4198
Arak Kanofsky Studios
610.330.9423
B. Designs
978.374.3575
Barbara Logan's Paperworks
301.774.2949
The Beverley Collection
904.387.2625

Blue Marmalade
877.597.2023
612.788.8517
Campbell Stationers & Engravers
214.692.8380
Cartier
212.753.0111
Claudia Laub Studio
323.931.1710
Cottage Industries
203.266.9075
Couturier de Cardboard
212.243.2225
Crane & Co. Papermakers
617.247.2822
Prudential Center
800 Boylston St.
Crane & Company
800.IS.CRANE
413.684.2600
www.crane.com
Creative Intelligence
323.936.9009
English Card Co.
516.520.6632
Enid Wilson
718.384.8814
Envelopments
714.258.2900
800.335.3536
The French Corner
800.421.4367
845.945.8414
www.frenchcorner.com
Hannah
847.864.8292

Hollis Hills Mill
718.217.4846
Hudon Street Papers
212.229.1064
I.H.M. Systems
516.589.5600
Index Print Media
212.979.6878
www.indexpm.com
Just Robin
310.273.9736
Kate's Paperie
212.941.9816
212.396.3670
212.633.0570
www.katespaperie.com
Katushka
206.632.3227
www.katushka.com
La Papeterie St-Armand
514.931.8338
100th Monkey Productions
818.398.3132
Mrs. John L. Strong
212.838.3848
Old Print Factory
800.325.5383
Orange Art
800.253.8975
Ordning & Reda
212.421.8199
The Paper Garden
210.494.9602
Paper Place
512.451.6531

Papivore
212.627.6055

Papyrus
800.355.8099
212.717.0002

Pendragon, Ink
508.234.6843

Printemps
203.226.6869

The Printery
516.922.3250

The Red Studio
323.465.2602

SoHo Letterpress
212.334.4356

Soho Reprographics
212.925.7575

Solum World Paper
650.812.7584
www.solum.com

Soolip Paperie & Press
310.360.0545

Twelve Dozen Graphics
617.363.9783

Uptown Rubber Stamps
970.493.3212
800.888.3212

Visual Miracles
212.691.4491

Viviano Design
503.973.6538
www.vivianodesign.com

The Wolf Paper & Twine Co.
212.675.4870

Write Selection
214.750.0531

Zorn Design
213.344.9995

TABLEWARE

Abigails
800.678.8485

Annie Glass
800.729.7350
www.annieglass.com

Arc International
800.257.7470

Buccellati
212.308.2900
310.276.702

Camden Lane
212.989.6813

Carnevale
800.548.9979
901.775.0800

Daniel Levy Ceramics
212.268.0878

Dansk International Designs Ltd.
800.293.2675
609.896.2800

Ebeling & Reuss
800.843.9551
610.366.8304

Fishs Eddy
877.347.4733
212.420.9020

Gense
888.368.4360
212.725.2882

Hoffman's Patterns of the Past
888.559.5335
815.875.1944

Lalique
800.993.2580
212.684.6760
www.lalique.com

Once Upon a Table
413.443.6622
www.onceuponatable.com

Ostafin Designs
212.352.9210

Potluck Studios
845.626.2300

Reed & Barton
800.822.1824
www.reedbarton.com

Rosenthal USA
800.804.8070
201.804.8000

Simon Pearce
212.334.2393
802.295.2711
www.simonpearce.com

WEDDING CAKES

Carol Schmidt
504.888.2049

Cheryl Kleinman
718.237.2271

Classic Cakes
317.844.6901

Classic Cakes and Pastries
860.586.8202

Cravings
314.961.3534

Culinary Institute of America
845.452.9600

Daniels Bakery
940.322.4043
Debra Yates
816.587.1095
Donald Wressel
310.273.2222
Duane Park Patisserie
888.274.8447
www.madelines.net
Edible Work of Art
312.895.2200
Fantasy Frostings
562.941.6266
800.649.0243
FJ Pastries
212.614.9054
Food Attitude
212.686.4644
www.weddingcakeonline.com
Frosted Art by Arturo Diaz
214.760.8707
Gail Watson Custom Cakes
212.967.9167
www.gailwatsoncake.com
Hansen Cakes
213.936.4332
Hirsch Baking
212.941.8085
Jan Kish
614.848.5855
Jan's Cakes
831.423.4481
Jane Stacey
505.473.1243
John and Mike's Amazing Cakes
206.869.2992

John Paul
843.744.6791
Le Gateau Cakery
214.528.6102
Les Friandises
212.988.1616
Michel Richard
310.275.5707
Mike's Amazing Cakes
425.869.2992
Patticakes
818.794.1128
A Piece of Cake
843.881.2034
Rosie's Creations
212.362.6069
Rosemary Watson
800.203.0629
201.538.3542
Rosemary's Cakes
201.833.2417
305.932.2989
Royale Icing Custom Cakes
708.386.4175
Sima's
414.257.0998
A Spirited Cake
214.522.2212
Steven Klc
703.848.0028
Susan Kennedy Chopson
615.865.2437

index

acknowledgements

I have been lucky enough to work with some of the best photographers in the business and they have played a big part in creating the beautiful pictures in this book. My heartfelt thanks to the following contributors:

Dan Duchars, Peter Durkes, Winfred Heinze, Janine Hosegood, Sian Irvine, Ray Main, JP Masclet, Bridget Peirson, Jonathon Russell Read, Pia Tryde, Jon Whitaker, Tim Winter, Theodore Wood
Brides and Homes/Planet Syndication

I would also like to thank three of my very favourite wedding photographers for their fabulous real-life weddings:

Lovegrove Photography
www.lovegrovephotography.co.uk
(pp 22–23/32–33/48–49,108–109)
Meg Smith www.megsmith.com
(pp 60–61/76–77, 92–93)
Stephen Swain
www.stephenswain.co.uk (pp 122–123)

Finally, a big thank-you to two of my *You & Your Wedding* team, Art Director Matt Inman and Style Editor, Kate Smallwood.